MW00441604

TOUGH CALLS

AN ILLUSTRATED BOOK OF
OFFICIAL BASEBALL RULES

Avon Books are available at special quantity discounts for bulk purchases for sales promotions, premiums, fund raising or educational use. Special books, or book excerpts, can also be created to fit specific needs.

For details write or telephone the office of the Director of Special Markets, Avon Books, Dept. FP, 1790 Broadway, New York, New York 10019, 212-399-1357.

TOUGH CALLS

AN ILLUSTRATED BOOK OF
OFFICIAL BASEBALL RULES

ZACH REBACKOFF

Illustrations by David Setlow

▲ AVON
PUBLISHERS OF BARD, CAMELOT, DISCUS AND FLARE BOOKS

TOUGH CALLS is an original publication of Avon Books. This work has never before appeared in book form.

AVON BOOKS
A division of
The Hearst Corporation
1790 Broadway
New York, New York 10019

Copyright © 1983, 1984 by Zach Rebackoff
Text design by Arlene Marin Pollard
Published by arrangement with the author
Library of Congress Catalog Card Number: 84-90892
ISBN: 0-380-86777-x

All rights reserved, which includes the right to reproduce this book or portions thereof in any form whatsoever except as provided by the U.S. Copyright Law. For information address Avon Books

First Avon Printing, May, 1984

AVON TRADEMARK REG. U. S. PAT. OFF. AND IN OTHER COUNTRIES, MARCA REGISTRADA, HECHO EN U. S. A.

Printed in the U. S. A.

DON   10   9   8   7   6   5   4   3   2   1

The Definitions of Terms and the captions for the illustrations in this book are excerpted from the *Official Baseball Rules*. Excerpts from the *Official Baseball Rules* reprinted by permission of the Commissioner of Baseball.

Interpretations and explanations of the Rules are the work of the author and are not part of the *Official Baseball Rules* nor are they endorsed by Baseball as an official interpretation.

Dedication

To all the players and managers who educated me (and those who tried, but failed to do so). In addition, my personal thanks to my friends and family, who helped by showing continued confidence in my creativity. I'm proud the list is too long to go through. However, they know who they are.

A special dedication belongs to my adorable daughter, Tara, who is starting to love baseball as much as her dolls. No special ruling could overrule my love and trust in her.

Table of Contents

Introduction

The last eight years of my life have been a long-running argument. If I wasn't arguing baseball with fellow umpires, I could certainly count on finding myself fighting to explain the rules to irate managers, coaches, players, fans and those indispensable, cheerleading trainers.

Everyone claims to know the rules better than anybody else. In addition, everyone is willing to share their wisdom with the umpire and then, of course, umpires don't always agree. Fortunately for my readers, I am what some would consider an expert. I became one the only possible way in baseball—the hard way—winning arguments and sometimes learning when I should have lost. For those readers who are not familiar with my background (which I hope is about a million of you), permit me to give you some relevant history.

Around 10 years ago, my life was that of a New York City cab driver. I was an aggressive individual, who had become eager for more creativity and direction. I didn't actually have that analyzed to this degree *then,* but nevertheless, that is the truth of the matter. Backtracking then, what future lay ahead in the path for a 23-year-old, 169-pound ball of hypertension?

The decision to elevate my life to an umpire was, of course, spontaneous. Baseball had always been in my blood. I felt it circulating again. An inadvertently serious suggestion was made by my long-time friend, Jimmy ("Musler") Doman. With an ordinary evening at hand, Jimmy sarcastically suggested that I respond to the television commercial "Be a Computer Trainee—Earn High Salary!!" Sorry, but that isn't exactly what I had in mind for the next 25 years.

With the next chilling TV episode on the back reel, Jimmy promoted another popular TV advertisement. "Truck Driver Training Institute" (Remember that one?). "Earn $300 a week." However, I just couldn't picture myself as this little head peering from the cab of a truck down a long, narrow highway. Besides, my bladder and kidneys had already been acutely strained during the last five "hacking" years.

Then, of course, came the ABC "Game of the Week" . . . or was it NBC? In any case, Jimmy stirred a reaction in me when he suggested I call balls and strikes. How could I not do that? The umpire gig sounded—and looked—quite challenging. I was immediately interested in pursuing the idea. After all, if it hadn't been for an elbow injury in high school football (Quarterback . . . all right, so it was the junior varsity.) I quite honestly believe I had some professional potential in my baseball game. In any case, I conducted a mini-investigation, applied, and attended the Bill Kinnamon Umpire School, in St. Petersburg, Fla.

I was assigned my first professional contract by the Class A Midwest League in April 1975. For those of you who are not familiar with the minor league baseball structure, here are a few basic points.

Each player, manager, coach, umpire, trainer, general manager or other front office worker is trying to promote himself through the basic three levels of the minor leagues: Classes A, AA and AAA (There are also several Class A Rookie Leagues, which are "short season" leagues for the very young and inexperienced pro.)

2

Nevertheless, the young umpire, or player, heads for his respective A league and begins the climb to reach the stadium they've always dreamt they'd homer in. (In my case, now, it was to peer through the big league pressure and crowd). Where? Hey, where else? Even strangers to New York want to "feel it" at Yankee Stadium. I mean, the Yankees have provided the world with the greatest team heroics in sports history. Think about it. Almost immediately however, my objectivity overwhelmed my previously biased Yankee loyalty.

"A" ball consists of approximately 10 leagues, with an average of eight teams in each league. Each of those teams is supported by a parent major league team.

Each league franchise supports a minor league team at each of the three minor league levels. For example, the New York Yankees' Class A affiliate is Fort Lauderdale, (Fla.), of the Florida State League, the Fort Lauderdale Yankees. The "AA" affiliate is the Nashville (Tenn.) Sounds of the Southern League, while the "AAA" club is the Columbus (Ohio) Clippers of the International League. There are three Double-A and three Triple-A leagues.

The immediate goal of the people holding the positions previously mentioned is to be promoted to AA, then to the AAA level. The next and final stop is—The Show!! So, in summation, each major league team has a group of men that is being groomed for their top club. Unfortunately, it doesn't always work out. Many more individuals fail than make it. All of the minor leagues are operated under the National Association of Professional Baseball Leagues.

Now, a quick flashback to the leagues I toiled in: 1975, Midwest League (A). 1976, Western Carolina League (A). 1977, Carolina League (A). 1978, Texas League (AA). 1979, International League (AAA). When I arrived in Columbus in May 1979, I couldn't believe the confines of Franklin County Stadium, the home of the Clippers. I swear I felt like I was in god-damned Yankee Stadium. Man, I was in AAA!! Wouldn't be long now. The last couple of years I had advanced rapidly, and was evidently considered a major league prospect.

I would say I was aggressive, perceptive, opinionated, clever, spontaneous, flamboyant, and neat, while all the time learning about life in the minors. My impression of the general consensus was that I had the respect of my colleagues, the players and managers. (Of course, a bad call, or what they *thought* was a bad call, could have led one to believe their opinion was otherwise.) I had learned to ease in and out of adversity with basic patience and common sense. That was rather new for me, as the first three years of my umpiring life were colored by stubbornness and self-gratification.

At the end of the 1979 campaign, I was advised by the Umpire Development Program that I was being given the opportunity to umpire in the Dominican Republic Winter League. Wow! Not only would this be exotic, but it very definitely indicated that I was a top minor league prospect. As a general rule, only the cream of the AAA umpires were selected, then contracted to work winter ball in either the Dominican Republic, Puerto Rico, or Venezuela.

The next season was a replay of the previous year, including the winter stint in the Dominican. Now, before I go any further, don't be misled that life in the minors was all peaches and cream—not by a long shot. Working in the minor leagues is no fun unless you're on the field. My constant six-month exposure to hotels, restaurants, never-ending car trips, fast food, my partner(s), loneliness, TV and one-night stands is not what I would call the Life of Riley. Nevertheless, I tried to make the best of this nightmare of suffering and trudged through. "When I reach the majors," I repeated over and over, "everything will be great." This Jewish kid from the Bronx was going to make his family and N.Y.C. proud of him.

My career flourished away from the night glare of the expressway to "el camino real," in Santo Domingo, where I conceived and directed the Zach Rebackoff Umpire School. This, the first major umpire school in the country's history, operates at the Olympic Center in the Dominican Republic's capital. By inducing large corporations to fund scholarships, in return for promotional considerations, the school has graduated 44 Dominican umpires. The demand for competent umpires was overwhelming in this

365-day-a-year baseball subculture. In essence, over my nine years of dedication, I progressed from the asphalt diamonds of 96th and 1st Ave. to become an ambitious and expressive contributor. I was, and still am, quite proud of my achievements (and my second language).

I must admit that umpiring in the minors does not have the glory and prestige that that major leagues offer. Nevertheless, the best part about umpiring in the minors was the never-ending moments of surprise . . . not to mention astonishment, embarrassment, boredom, anger, and last but not least, achievement. Hey, you know what was really fun? Seeing, meeting, then working alongside bonafide baseball celebrities. Of course, upon first meeting people they have only read about or seen on TV, most people try to make light of the moment, or make it look quite routine. However, we mere mortals, who are not inhibited, do find ourselves caught up in the radiance that the luminaries carry with them. Wouldn't you find it hard not to be momentarily captivated by the aura of the stars?

Hey, once I was so psyched up for my first home plate meeting with Earl Weaver, that when I finally arrived at the pre-game meeting, I surprised everyone, most of all Earl, by putting out my palm and blurting out, "All right, Earl Weaver, gimme five" — and he did! I know that kind of behavior is considered 'gosh-wow' and spontaneous, but so what? I felt great! Must one be consistently constrained? Feeling great is what life is all about. Of course, after working for and with these stars of the past and present, their presence becomes quite natural, and their insults are handled in the same fashion as everyone else's.

When you familiarize yourself with the contents of *Tough Calls* you will be amazed at how much humor is camouflaged by the apparently regimented image the professional game presents. About 98 percent of the time, the fans cannot really hear what is said on the field by the participants. For example, in your honest opinion, could you imagine this specific case.

Yogi Berra's son, Dale, came up through the minors with me. "Little Yogi" was one of my favorite antagonists. He is from New Jersey, but was so New Yorkish that we would banter about anything . . . just to feel like we were back in New York! Dale made me laugh.

Berra was coming to bat one afternoon in Charleston, S.C. The opposition was making a pitching change, so Dale and I moved off to the side of home plate to chat.

"So what're your plans for the winter?," Dale started.

"I'm going to live in New York and probably drive a cab again. Would love to catch the World Series if the Yankees are in. Hey, that reminds me, Dale, do you get tickets?"

Dale confidently replied, "Sure. Why, you want tickets?"

"Sure", I confirmed, "I'd love to go."

"O.K. When the series rolls around, look me up and I'll get 'em for you."

"Great," I exclaimed, "I'll do just that." After a short contemplation, I continued. "Hey, are you just blowing smoke or are you guaranteeing me the seats?

"Listen, Zach," Dale retorted, clearing the air of uncertainty. "If I want tickets, I get tickets!!" I had to feel confident; after all, his father *was* Yogi Berra.

The reliever finished up his warm-up tosses and everybody stepped into position ready for action. There were two outs and runners on first and second as Dale ran the count to 2-2. I found myself, at this time, hoping Dale *would not* look at a called third strike. Damned if a sharp-breaking slider didn't catch Dale looking, and I banged him out on strikes. I cannot swear the pitch was a strike. As a matter of fact, thinking back now, the pitch was probably 4 inches outside! I can only account for my enlarged strike zone with this answer. I feel that I momentarily placed myself on a much too personal level with Dale, and was consequently influenced (subconsciously) by the 60-second verbal exchange. The other side of the coin would have been to call the pitch a ball, risking Dale to believe he was reprieved because of the ticket fantasy.

Nevertheless, Dale was obviously ticked off and let me know it. He ripped off his helmet and discarded it along with his bat. He started to move toward his defensive position at third base, but not before stating his final words in the New York accent I was so familiar with. "Tickets, Zach, you want tickets? Yeah, you'll get tickets. Why don't you start holding your breath *now* so you can pass out and dream you have box seats!"

When I was making judgments out on the baseball field the public had no choice but to accept and sometimes weep over my decisions. Why I have the audacity to believe that my thoughts and interpretations are still important is beyond me, except for the fact that I really have dissected the official baseball rules and have some rather surprising findings. I have experienced working in a two, three, four and six-man unpiring system and have probed each for flaws and advantages.

The official rules are used internationally by all professional leagues and most amateurs (with modification). The same rule book is used for the entire professional structure. These rules are not to be modified in any way, to be in conflict or contrary to the actual rules in question (there are, in the Major Leagues, an addition to these rules which is a properly named manual called *Special Instructions to Umpires.)* The manual contains precise rule interpretations and modifications of the rules that are "problematic." Big league umpires occasionally encounter unusual game and stadium conditions that make these special instructions relevant.

At that very moment of this writing, I am in the midst of opening the largest and most complete umpire training facility in the country, based in New York's metropolitan area. "The New York School of Umpiring," under the direction of yours truly, will operate during the spring and summer months. The school is open to all who are interested in this unique profession, and that includes women! (Information and brochures may be obtained by writing to: N.Y. School of Umpiring, P.O. Box 1226, Riverdale, N.Y. 10471).

In researching this book project, I found myself extremely interested in how the rules of baseball were actually formed. After all, who actually conceived the initial guidelines for the game? The results of my findings were surprising. For example, who invented the game of baseball? Abner Doubleday? Wrong. In 1839, Doubleday was instrumental in creating a game called "town ball."

This game was initially started in London. The contest was played with a 4-inch flat board for a bat, and the pitcher stood only 50 feet from the home base. Each base was 50 feet from the other. Doubleday cannot take credit for the invention of baseball, as this game of town ball evolved from an even earlier game called "rounders." The game was eventually played the same as town ball minus the 4-inch flat board. Runners could be put out by being "plunked" (hit by a thrown ball).

In 1839, the word *diamond* was first used in print in the *Boys Book of Sports*. Doubleday did suggest the use of 11 players to a team, but did not originate the team system.

In the 1880s, umpires were granted absolute authority when presiding over professional games. Arguing in the smallest degree was not tolerated. A player was not allowed to leave his position to question the umpire. This was considered a severe violation of the rules and an instant fine was imposed—by the umpire himself! Fines of $5 to $25 were assessed any participant who delayed the game by arguing. (I like that!).

In continuing my research, I learned that home plate was not used to determine balls and strikes. If the umpire believed the pitch was in a legitimate hitting area, and the "striker" did not swing, it would be ruled a strike. The shoulder was the height limit. Rule 43, Section 8 of the *Baseball Manual* by Henry Chadwick described many unusual rules that we have discarded since the game has progressed. One of them was intentionally fouling off a pitch with the count of 2 strikes. This act would prompt the umpire to rule "Strike 3, the batter's out." So much for trying to hang in there.

Our rules expert of that time period was one Henry Chadwick, also known as "Father Baseball." Chadwick was the game's original play master. Henry wrote the first books for The Spaulding Collection on the art of pitching, batting and fielding which were all included together with the rules in the *Baseball Manual*. These scriptures have been put on microfilm and can be found at the New York Public Library. The series of books cannot give you the exact year of print as some pages either had been mutilated or are missing. It has taken me many hours to examine the microfilm and determine which pages were part of each of the five books included on record. The microfilm states that at the time the film was put together, pages and covers to the relics were missing, or mutilated. However, I found the missing material would be added or inserted at their proper places or at the end of the reel. Since there were five books to contend with, I was confused at times as to what page was from which book. In any case, the relevancy here is that these writings were formed to create the foundation and integrity of professional baseball. Chadwick was obviously the main baseball authority of the era, and led the original Rules Committee to attain the proper perspective of the game.

It is interesting to note that there were two sets of baseball manuals presented on this microfilm. The total series is represented by "The Spaulding Collection," while there is also a fairly legible set of rules which is called, simply, *The Baseball Manual.* The manual's introduction emphasizes that because of the growth in baseball's popularity, a major change took place from 1857–1871. In 1857, the only professionalism baseball could claim was the "National Association of Baseball Players." This association conducted its game with a set of rules set forth by the organization in question. In 1881, however, spurred by baseball's increasing popularity and the introduction of a class of trained professionals attached to a stock company, two national associations were formed: the Major Leagues and the Minor Leagues, both conforming to the same code of rules.

The original baseball manual contained much more than the playing rules. It provided information on the following areas: playing each position, scoring rules, field dimensions, diagrams and how to report on the game. I tend to agree with the book's title, *The Baseball Manual.* It really gave you an in-depth and overall picture of the game. In addition, the book contained a glossary of the game's terms. They were primitive, yet somewhat inventive just the same. Of course, it is only logical to assume that the game's innovators were presented with vocabulary dilemmas, as never before were baseball terms, and phrases, used in such a technical and definitive way. It's amazing how a few of the terms and phrases have continued to be excellent choices. Other words or terms have also remained, but have taken on new meaning. (For example, the word *strike*. In those days it meant *to swing*. Now it is, of course, part of the batter's ball and strike count.) How about *blind?* For all of us now, we can logically assume we're talking about the umpire—"He's blind." Chadwick had other ideas. The term meant a blank score. I'm going to list just a few contrasts between today's vocabulary and that of the 1880s. I'm sure you'll find them interesting.

Baseball Manual 188? (Date Mutilated)

1) *Bases*—12-inch square.
2) *Homeplate*—12-inch square made of marble or stone, with one of the 4 points facing the pitcher's plate.

3) *Pitcher's Box*—6-foot square—front line 45 ft. from center of H.P. (home plate).

4) *Batter's Box*—3 inch x 6 inch-1 ft. from sides of H.P.
5) *Ball*—Out of striker's legitimate reach.
6) *Dropping the Pace*—Pitcher lessens his speed of his delivery and substitutes a medium-paced ball for a swift one.
7) *Headwork*—Pitcher *adds* judgement to aid his physical skills.
8) *Punishing the Pitcher*—Getting a lot of hits off the pitcher
9) *Wides*—Balls pitched beyond the legitimate reach of the bat

1983 Official Baseball Rules and Modern Terminology

1) *Bases*—15 inch square
2) *Home Plate*—17 inch front edge, made of rubber.

3) *Pitcher's Mound*—18-feet diameter, the rubber being 60 feet 6 inches from the back of H.P.
4) *Batter's Box*—4 feet x 6 feet-6 inches from the side of H.P.
5) *Ball*—Pitch not entering the strike zone.
6) *Changeup*—A windup which appears faster than it is, forcing the batter to be off stride for the off-speed pitch.
7) *Brains*—Logic

8) *Getting Killed*—Banging the ball all over the place (by the opposition)
9) *Ball*—Pitch out of the strike zone.

In addition to these terms, a number of rules that attracted my attention were: three balls gave a runner 1st base, rather than the four we now use; baserunners were called safe if the play was a tie. (Umpires in todays game usually abide by this unwritten rule. However, this rule was *written* right into the manual!).

Fan interference was a *laugh.* When the ball entered the spectator area, the ball had to be located and brought back to the pitcher's box before anyone could be put out or have time called. Another oddity was that players could position themselves in foul territory. The reason was that balls that hit in fair territory initially would be ruled fair balls—even if they ended upon foul territory before passing first or third base. Relief pitchers were permitted, but they could only come from the starting nine. This prompted managers to have their relief ace play in the outfield so he would be rested if needed in an emergency.

In any case, this book contains 50 situations that can be confusing even to players and fans of this modern era. You won't be disappointed with this book. You might be surprised, even amazed by the situations and solutions presented between the covers. I've lived and ruled through a great many of them, keeping in mind the old baseball saying: "You never know."

This book will teach you about baseball in a unique, insider's way. Bring it to games, entertain and impress your guests, the local sports know-it-alls or just sit back and enjoy a new slant on America's greatest entertainment.

I would like to add that on occasion, throughout the *Tough Calls,* I make references to actual people, places and plays that I have encountered or witnessed personally—or have attained knowledge of by research. By no means have I intended to discredit or embarrass any individual. The opinions and interpretations that are expressed between these covers are totally my own and should not be confused with those of the Baseball Commissioner's Office or either the Major or Minor Leagues, unless specifically stated to the contrary.

2.00 — Definitions of Terms. (Excerpts from the 1983 Official Baseball Rules)

An **APPEAL** is the act of a fielder in claiming violation of the rules by the offensive team.

A **BALK** is an illegal act by the pitcher with a runner or runners on base, entitling all runners to advance one base.

A **BALL** is a pitch which does not enter the strike zone in flight and is not struck at by the batter.

BATTER-RUNNER is a term that identifies the offensive player who has just finished his time at bat until he is put out or until the play on which he became a runner ends.

The **BATTERY** is the pitcher and catcher.

BENCH OR DUGOUT is the seating facilities reserved for players, substitutes and other team members in uniform when they are not actively engaged on the playing field.

A **BUNT** is a batted ball not swung at, but intentionally met with the bat and tapped slowly within the infield.

A **CALLED GAME** is one in which, for any reason, the umpire-in-chief terminates play.

A **CATCH** is the act of a fielder in getting secure possession in his hand or glove of a ball in flight and firmly holding it; providing he does not use his cap, protector, pocket or any other part of his uniform in getting possession. It is not a catch, however, if simultaneously or immediately following his contact with the ball, he collides with a player, or with a wall, or if he falls down, and as a result of such collision or falling, drops the ball. It is not a catch if a fielder touches a fly ball which then hits a member of the offensive team or an umpire and then is caught by another defensive player. If the fielder has made the catch and drops the ball while in the act of making a throw following the catch, the ball shall be adjudged to have been caught. In establishing the validity of the catch, the fielder shall hold the ball long enough to prove that he has complete control of the ball and that his release of the ball is voluntary and intentional.

A catch is legal if the ball is finally held by any fielder, even though juggled, or held by another fielder before it touches the ground. Runners may leave their bases the instant the first fielder touches the ball. A fielder may reach over a fence, railing, rope or other line of demarcation to make a catch. He may jump on top of a railing, or canvas that may be in foul ground. No interference should be allowed when a fielder reaches over a fence, railing, rope or into a stand to catch a ball. He does so at his own risk.

13

If a fielder, attempting a catch at the edge of the dugout, is "held up" and kept from an apparent fall by a player or players of either team and the catch is made, it shall be allowed.

THE **CATCHER'S BOX** is that area within which the catcher shall stand until the pitcher delivers the ball.

A **DEAD BALL** is a ball out of play because of a legally created temporary suspension of play.

A **DOUBLE-HEADER** is two regularly scheduled or rescheduled games, played in immediate succession.

A **DOUBLE PLAY** is a play by the defense in which two offensive players are put out as a result of continuous action, providing there is no error between putouts.

(a) A force double play is one in which both putouts are force plays.

(b) A reverse force double play is one in which the first out is a force play and the second out is made on a runner for whom the force is removed the reason of the first out. Examples of reverse force plays: runner on first, one out; batter grounds to first baseman, who steps on first base (one out) and throws to second baseman or shortstop for the second out (a tag play).

Another example: bases loaded, none out; batter grounds to third baseman, who steps on third base (one out), then throws to catcher for the second out (tag play).

A **FAIR BALL** is a batted ball that settles on fair ground between home and first base, or between home and third base, or that is on or over fair territory when bounding to the outfield past first or third base, or that touches first, second or third base, or that first falls on fair territory on or beyond first base or third base, or that, while on or over fair territory, touches the person of an umpire or player, or that, while over fair territory, passes out of the playing field in flight.

FIELDER'S CHOICE is the act of a fielder who handles a fair grounder and, instead of throwing to first base to put out the batter-runner, throws to another base in an attempt to put out a preceding runner. The term is also used by scorers (a) to account for the advance of the batter-runner who takes one or more extra bases when the fielder who handles his safe hit attempts to put out a preceding runner; (b) to account for the advance of a runner (other than by stolen base or error) while a fielder is attempting to put out another runner; and (c) to account for the advance of a runner made solely because of the defensive team's indifference (undefended steal).

A **FORCE PLAY** is a play in which a runner legally loses his right to occupy a base by reason of the batter becoming a runner.

Confusion regarding this play is removed by remembering that frequently the "force" situation is removed during the play. Example: Man on first, one out, ball hit sharply to first baseman who touches the bag and batter-runner is out. The force is removed at that moment and runner advancing to second must be tagged. If there had been a runner on third or second, and either of these runners scored before the tag-out at second, the run counts. Had the first baseman thrown to second and the ball then had been returned to first, the play at second was a force out, making two outs, and the return throw to first ahead of the runner would have made three outs. In that case, no run would score.

EXAMPLE: Not a force out. One out. Runner on first and third. Batter flies out. Two out. Runner on third tags up and scores. Runner on first tries to retouch before throw from fielder reaches first baseman, but does not get back in time and is out. Three outs. If, in umpire's judgment, the runner from third touched home before the ball was held at first base, the run counts.

A **FORFEITED GAME** is a game declared ended by the umpire-in-chief in favor of the offended team by the score of 9 to 0, for violation of the rules.

A **FOUL BALL** is a batted ball that settles on foul territory between home and first base, or between home and third base, or that bounds past first or third base on or over foul territory, or that first falls on foul territory beyond first or third base, or that, while on or over foul territory, touches the person of an umpire or player, or any object foreign to the natural ground.

A **FOUL TIP** is a batted ball that goes sharp and direct from the bat to the catcher's hands and is legally caught. It is not a foul tip unless caught and any foul tip that is caught is a strike, and the ball is in play. It is not a catch if it is a rebound, unless the ball has first touched the catcher's glove or hand.

The **HOME TEAM** is the team on whose grounds the game is played, or if the game is played on neutral grounds, the home team shall be designated by mutual agreement.

An **ILLEGAL PITCH** is (1) a pitch delivered to the batter when the pitcher does not have his pivot foot in contact with the pitcher's plate; (2) a quick return pitch. An illegal pitch when runners are on base is a balk.

IN FLIGHT describes a batted, thrown, or pitched ball which has not yet touched the ground or some object other than a fielder.

IN JEOPARDY is a term indicating that the ball is in play and an offensive player may be put out.

An **INNING** is that portion of a game within which the teams alternate on offense and defense and in which there are three putouts for each team. Each team's time at bat is a half-inning.

LEGAL (or **LEGALLY**) is in accordance with these rules.

A **LIVE BALL** is a ball which is in play.

A **LINE DRIVE** is a batted ball that goes sharp and direct from the bat to a fielder without touching the ground.

THE **MANAGER** is a person appointed by the club to be responsible for the team's actions on the field, and to represent the team in communications with the umpire and the opposing team. A player may be appointed manager.

(a) The club shall designate the manager to the league president or the umpire-in-chief not less than thirty minutes before the scheduled starting time of the game.

(b) The manager may advise the umpire that he has delegated specific duties prescribed by the rules to a player or coach, and any action of such designated representative shall be official. The manager shall always be responsible for his team's conduct, observance of the official rules, and deference to the umpires.

(c) If a manager leaves the field, he shall designate a player or coach as his substitute, and such substitute manager shall have the duties, rights and responsibilities of the manager. If the manager fails or refuses to designate his substitute before leaving, the umpire-in-chief shall designate a team member as substitute manager.

OBSTRUCTION is the act of a fielder who, while not in possession of the ball and not in the act of fielding the ball, impedes the progress of any runner.

OFFENSE is the team, or any player of the team, at bat.

The **PERSON** of a player or an umpire is any part of his body, his clothing or his equipment.

A **PITCH** is a ball delivered to the batter by the pitcher. All other deliveries of the ball by one player to another are thrown balls.

A **PITCHER** is the fielder designated to deliver the pitch to the batter.

The pitcher's **PIVOT FOOT** is that foot which is in contact with the pitcher's plate as he delivers the pitch.

"PLAY" is the umpire's order to start the game or to resume action following any dead ball.

A **RETOUCH** is the act of a runner in returning to a base as legally required.

A **RUN** (or **SCORE**) is the score made by an offensive player who advances from batter to runner and touches first, second, third and home bases in that order.

A **RUN-DOWN** is the act of the defense in an attempt to put out a runner between bases.

"SAFE" is a declaration by the umpire that a runner is entitled to the base for which he was trying.

SET POSITION is one of the two legal pitching positions.

SQUEEZE PLAY is a term to designate a play when a team, with a runner on third base, attempts to score that runner by means of a bunt.

The **STRIKE ZONE** is that space over home plate which is between the batter's armpits and the top of his knees when he assumes his natural stance. The umpire shall determine the strike zone according to the batter's usual stance when he swings at a pitch.

A **SUSPENDED GAME** is a called game which is to be completed at a later date.

A **TAG** is the action of a fielder in touching a base with his body while holding the ball securely and firmly in his hand or glove; or touching a runner with the ball, or with his hand or glove holding the ball, while holding the ball securely and firmly in his hand or glove.

A **TIE GAME** is a regulation game which is called when each team has the same number of runs.

"TIME" is the announcement by an umpire of a legal interruption of play, during which the ball is dead.

A **TRIPLE PLAY** is a play by the defense in which three offensive players are put out as a result of continuous action, providing there is no error between putouts.

A **WILD PITCH** is one so high, so low, or so wide of the plate that it cannot be handled with ordinary effort by the catcher.

WIND-UP POSITION is one of the two legal pitching positions.

FIELD AND EQUIPMENT

Cut Ball
Rule 3.02

A solid piece of advice was once bestowed upon me at the Bill Kinnamon Umpire School: "Don't look for trouble out there; trouble will find you." No truer words have ever been repeated.

But what if the batter asks the umpire to examine the ball? Happens every game. So you look at it, and there it is, *cut*. No blade of grass did that. The devilish antics of a shrewd defensive player are evident here. Probably the pitcher, but not definitely. Maybe the catcher or any one of the infielders. Ever try to hit a slider at 90 mph? Aside from a good knuckleball that's the toughest pitch to hit. An experienced flick of the wrist can cause a sudden change of direction in a ball that is at times, unfollowable. A cut ball? Hey, even the pitcher himself couldn't predict the last moments of insanity the ball will exhibit.

But men will be men and try anything to create adversity on the diamond. The trick is not commonplace, but does occur occasionally. Our umpire must act with control, tact, diplomacy and, most of all, integrity.

In ejecting a player or pitcher in this situation the umpire should be aware of the adverse reaction he will experience when he does actually declare his ruling. With baseball salaries as they are

Cut Ball
Rule 3.02

3.02 No player shall intentionally discolor or damage the ball by rubbing it with soil, rosin, paraffin, licorice, sand paper, emery paper or other foreign substance.

PENALTY: The umpire shall demand the ball and remove the offender from the game. In case the umpire cannot locate the offender, and if the pitcher delivers such discolored or damaged ball to the batter, the pitcher shall be removed from the game at once and shall be suspended automatically for ten days.

today, 10 days pay is a nice piece of change. Ejections get people angry, and the angrier they get, the more the ejection will cost them. Our responsible umpire is most likely in for a heated argument, and will surely be scrutinized for his ruling.

So the question is: Does the umpire simply make light of the hitters request to examine the cut ball, hide it from the batter, and put a new ball in play—or does he do his job and investigate? Me? I'm out there investigating, because I'm supposed to enforce the rules, not overlook them!

Pitcher's Mound

The mound, or "hill" if you wish, is the pampered pet of the grounds crew. It is in constant need of daily massages to maintain the pinpoint dimensions that it follows. After learning the mound's specifics such as diameter, circumference, etc., I believed every mound thereafter would look and be the same. Obviously from my commentary, you can bet I'm going to make you as I am now, a non-believer.

It is true that each mound maintains the proportional measures set forth in the rule book. However, one particular *"mound... tain"* I personally peered over made me skeptical. That was the giant hill at Wall Powell Park in Charleston, W. Va.

The field is situated in a beautiful valley, surrounded by the pine tree-filled mountains of the Kanowha Valley. To see the mountains from behind home plate, it was apparent that this sight was an outstanding background for the hitters. My first appearance in Charleston was an experience in itself, and more so when I arrived at home plate. Something appeared odd, yet I could not

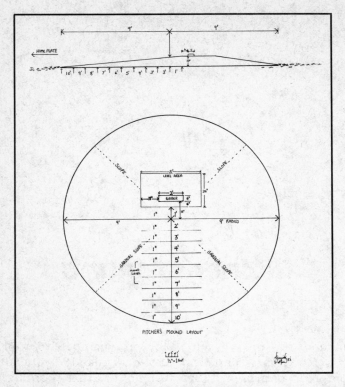

Pitcher's Mound
Diagram No. 3—Official Baseball Rules

DIAGRAM NO. 3 The degree of slope from a point 6″ in front of the pitcher's plate to a point 6′ toward home plate be 1″ to 1′, and such degree of slope shall be uniform.

Pitching Mound—An 18′ diameter circle, center of which is 59′ from back of home plate.

Locate front edge of rubber 18″ behind center of mound.

Front edge of rubber to back point of home plate, 60′6″.

Slope starts 6″ from front edge of rubber.

Slope shall be 6″ from starting point, 6″ in front of rubber to point 6′ in front of rubber, and slope shall be uniform.

Level area surrounding rubber should be 6″ in front of rubber, 18″ to each side and 22″ to rear of rubber. Total level area 5′ x 34″

put my finger on it. By the end of the first inning, I realized what seemed so unusual. A mini-mountain was protruding from the center of the infield! I mean the pitcher looked like he was 20 feet tall!

This mound had to be illegal. I knew it! In all the years I have been around baseball, each mound I saw might appear slightly different from the next; however, all had consistency in relation to height. The mound at Watt Powell? One might need a *cab* to make the hill?

Dissecting the terminology used in the illustration, you will notice a series of specifics a mound must conform to. It is possible that one might be confused when trying to understand how the degree of slope is measured. To make it easier, imagine yourself on the top of the hill. From a level area 6 inches in front of you toward home plate, walk directly toward the plate. You will encounter a gradual slope. Every 12 inches you move closer, you lose 1 inch of height. Finally, after moving 10 feet from the level ground on top, you are now, or should be, 10 inches shorter.

One dimension of the mound that I initially found surprising is the pitcher's rubber—6 x 24 inches. That is quite a slab when you think about it. It doesn't appear that big when you watch a game on TV. The pitcher *does not* have to place his pivot foot on top of the rubber when he delivers. A traditional hole is dug out by both starters and each pitcher pivots out of the hole while making contact with the rubber's front edge with the back side of their shoes. Using the trench in front, the pitcher can push off and therefore gain more velocity and control. According to the specifics laid out in the book, the pitcher will be firing from a point higher than ground level of course.

That brings us back to Charleston. If that mound was prepared to station the pitcher 10 inches above the level surface of the field, then I'll send their chief groundskeeper a free copy of this book— and a personal apology, as well! I've never measured that mound—or any other for that matter,—but whenever I busted up a conference on the Charleston mound, the entire trip up and down made me wish it was "Miller Time."

Umpires Observe Unlined Portion of Foul Line

Rule 3.01B

This section of text will examine a portion of the rule book that can be expected to only apply in a professional ball park. Foul lines (which of course should be renamed *fair lines*) and the batter's box lines can only be expected to be laid out by professional clubs. Amateur and other organized leagues can only *hope* to afford the luxury of good playing fields, a grounds crew and, of course, lime.

The home club cannot really consider itself a class operation if the field's most important set of boundaries are not clearly and visibly established. Therefore, the umpire's meeting at home plate before the game is the place to re-evaluate any field irregularities or inconsistencies. If a verbal agreement is to be made, that is the place and time to do it. However, I cannot visualize the following conversation:

"Well, I guess since we're missing about 20 feet of the foul line, we'll just go by *our* judgment."

"Sure Zach," say the two managers in unison, "Let's get going."

First of all, the umpires do not have to put themselves at a greater disadvantage than they already are. Number two, what reason could there be for starting the game without reasonably resolving the foul line problem? In my opinion, it would be a lack

**Umpires Observe Unlined Portion of Foul Line
Rule 3.01 (b)**

3.01 Before the game begins the umpire shall—

(b) Be sure that all playing lines (heavy lines on Diagrams No. 1 and No. 2) are marked with lime, chalk or other white material easily distinguishable from the ground or grass.

of fortitude. There it is, right in front of them, too!

The grounds crew evidently lost its stroke and no one noticed the missing lime until game time. To resolve the problem would only take two minutes! Have them return to the foul line and fill in the missing 20 feet. That's a very easy decision until the grounds crew informs the time-conscious umpires that they had run out of lime and it would take 30–45 minutes to locate more of the substance and lay it down. Now you're talking dilemma. The starting pitchers have just finished their pre-game warm-up and their arms will stiffen if the game does not commence on schedule. The visiting team has grounds for a protest! Not that they are the favorite to win it, but they can make a valid claim.

I can relate to game preliminaries in a rather odd way. I've experienced a protest because the scheduled starting time was passed by and then protested. It happened this way.

The site was Salem, Va., where Jack Aker's Mets were visiting Steve Demeter's Pirates. I rate this stadium in the top ten worst I had ever raised my right arm in. It was set way down from ground level and reminded me of a pit for ancient gladiators. It was always 100° in the shade and our locker room was a giant 6-foot by 9-foot hole atop the field. Today's game was to follow a pre-game promo of *cow milking!* The contest was running late, and the Pirates G.M. (general manager) knocked on our door about five minutes before game time. He advised us (my partner Mike Bender and I) that an additional 20 minutes would be extended to finish up the crowdpleasing cow milking contest. "Fine," Mike said, "Have you advised both managers?" The G.M. told us "Yeah, sure, we're telling them now."

And that was that until we got the word that the field was clear and the game was ready to begin. Nothing was said at home plate in reference to protesting the late start. Jack, Steve, Mike and I merely repeated that we were all annoyed at the delay, but since this was *a ball* we had to put up with it.

The Pirates immediately proceeded to light up the Met hurler for five runs in the first inning. After the inning, Aker strolled out of his dugout to visit me at home plate.

Calmly and diligently, Aker started, "Zach, I'm officially

protesting this game.''

"Now?'' I argued.

"Yep, now,'' Jack responded.

"For what, Jack? Because the guy got lit up for five runs and now you're going to blame his bad outing on the delay?''

Jack again calmly replied, "Yep.''

"You can't protest, Jack; it's too late. You should have said something before we started.''

Jack just looked me straight in the eye and calmly and irreversably said, "I'm protesting . . . now, right now! And you are going to handle it, too!''

The game preliminaries raced through my mind. I concluded I had nothing to lose by announcing the protest. It's his club's money! (It costs a certain amount for a team to lodge a protest). I called Mike down from first base and gave him the scoop. Mike agreed with my reasoning, and really saw no problem in announcing Jack's protest. Did we have a choice? However, in the back of our minds we wondered if somehow *we* had screwed up and could lose the protest. In view of the circumstances, the league did not uphold the protest, and the game was ruled official.

This is an example of how a seemingly meaningless situation can brew into an official protest. We really had our hands tied when the delay was announced. What were we to do, push the cows off the field? Being in only my second year of pro ball did not help matters much either, as this was the first time I'd encountered a protest over game preliminaries.

Now, let's get back to our illustrated problem of the chalk line. Fortunately for me, my subconscious solves many of my daily situations. My gut feeling is to *not* feel inhibited in asking for a delay when I am responsible for the playing of the game and the maintenance of the rules. Why rush? Take a few seconds to consult with your partners. Perhaps a stroke of white paint would suffice until the lime could be delivered. This antidote would only set back the starting time 10 minutes, at the most! That decision deserves the claim of ingenuity and improvisation. No white paint??? Well, then, let's wait for the lime, and hope that both teams and the fans understand.

Field Layout
(Diagram No. 2—Official Baseball Rules)

No matter how much you think you know regarding the actual field dimensions of a baseball diamond, I am sure a few of the numbers you see in the illustration will surprise you. For instance, the distance between the batter's box and home plate. For some reason, I always believed the distance was greater than 6 inches. Or how about the distance from the pitcher's rubber to home plate. If I asked 10 people I'm sure 9 out of the 10 would say 60 feet. Again, 6 inches comes into play . . . and remember, it is measured from the front edge of the pitcher's rubber to the point of home plate.

The 15 inch-square bases are interesting to note, as well. I've always felt that the bases should be a couple of inches wider for plays that develop with the defense and the offense both wanting a piece of the bag at the same time, resulting in a spike injury which gives a player a nasty gash and stitches. As indicated by the size difference since the original creation of the bases, the lords of baseball had previously dealt with this very suggestion.

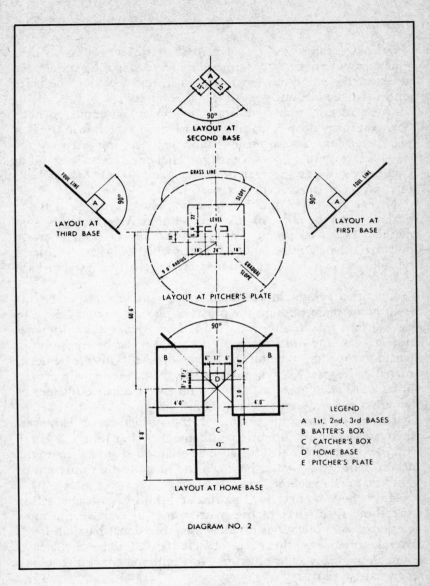

LAYOUT AT
SECOND BASE

LAYOUT AT
THIRD BASE

GRASS LINE

LAYOUT AT
FIRST BASE

LAYOUT AT PITCHER'S PLATE

LEGEND

A 1st, 2nd, 3rd BASES
B BATTER'S BOX
C CATCHER'S BOX
D HOME BASE
E PITCHER'S PLATE

LAYOUT AT HOME BASE

DIAGRAM NO. 2

**Field Layout
Diagram No. 2**

When the game was first played back in the late 1800s, 12-inch-square bases were used. I assume that before long the gentlemanly aspect of the game was left in the dust, and blocking the bases with whatever ingenuity possible was adopted.

One particular note here is a little-known fact about catcher's box. Not many people can claim knowledge of the box in the first place, let alone the surprising dimension. As indicated by the arrows and markings, you can see the catcher can actually stand or crouch as close as the rear of home plate. (Look for catcher's interference when he gets that close.)

My favorite trivia question regarding the playing field is the distance from the home plate to second base. Anyone with a solid mathematical background would get the answer from knowing only that the field was a 90-ft. sq. For us who need it made easier, I can tell you it is 127 feet, 3⅜ inches. Try that one at your local tavern!

It is also suggested in the rules that the field be set so that a line from home plate through the pitcher's plate to second base runs east-northeast. Without having a lot of knowledge about the solar system, I assume this suggestion is based on the best position in regard to the sun's glare for the hitters. (To hell with the fielders.) Actually, I agree with the idea of the park design helping the hitter's vision. Otherwise, they would be in constant danger of being seriously injured.

There is no maximum distance to the outfield fence. However, there are minumum distance requirements. After June 1, 1959, a stipulation was made that distance be established at 325 feet to the nearest fence (that would be down the lines) and a minimum of 400 feet to dead center.

Meanwhile, it's uncanny that first and third base coaches refuse to confine themselves to the coach's box. They have the most spacious accommodations of all. Most professional baseball fields are manicured expertly and to observe the full scope of the field from atop is really a great picture. Next time you go, you're sure to see what I mean.

Foreign Substance
Rule 8.02B

Unfortunately, umpires are not trained in detective work, yet a crash course wouldn't be a bad idea. It is highly unlikely that the brief course would come in handy on a daily basis, but occasionally the tact and discretion would serve its purpose.

In 1979, my first season in AAA, Greg Henley and Jack Lietz were my partners in crime. As a fresh young rookie out of the AA ranks, I had the ambition and desire to conquer the world—and the rules. I had no interest in police work, never mind handling detective assignments. One particular evening *there was a detective* occupying a seat in the Columbus Clipper dugout. His name was Stan Williams. Williams had previously masqueraded as the Columbus pitching coach! Let me set the scene for you.

The Clippers were hosting the Chiefs from Syracuse on a balmy night at Franklin County Stadium. Greg was calling balls and strikes, Jack was manning first base, and I was contemplating dinner at third. The Clippers were up to bat with Gene Michael managing the hard-hitting Yankee farm club from the third base coaching box. The Yankees, as you might know, go first class throughout their entire organization. With this in mind, it is not surprising that the Clippers had all kinds of coaches, ranging from hitting to fielding to pitching, not to mention video equipment

Foreign Substance
Rule 8.02 (b)

8.02 The pitcher shall not—

(b) Have on his person, or in his possession, any foreign substance. For such infraction of this section (b) the penalty shall be immediate ejection from the game.

(another coach handled that) and last, but *not* least, a designated bullpen catcher. To make it simple, Michael's job was comparatively easy compared to other AAA managers who were *lucky* to have a pitching coach, period! So there stood Gene, conjuring up secret signals, as his braintrust countered by observing from the dugout.

With the game moving along at a routine pace, Stan Williams bursts out of the dugout, right smack in the middle of a hitter's turn at bat. He requested time and proceeded to home plate to chat with Henley. After they exchanged a few words, Henley started out to the mound. Vern Benson, the Chiefs' manager, realizing something was not kosher, joined the conference on the mound, as did the Chiefs' catcher. From the third base foul line I couldn't understand what they were talking about. Mike Willis, the Chiefs' pitcher, had previously been up in "The Show" and I pondered what a big leaguer like Willis was scrutinized for. The suspense was overwhelming so I paid a visit as well—just to learn, of course.

When I got there, I heard this conversation:

HENLEY: "Okay Mike, you're done!"

BENSON: "What for?"

ME: "Yeah, Greg, what for??"

HENLEY: "He's got pine tar on his forearm."

BENSON: "Oh, come on, Greg, he must have bumped into a bat in the dugout and didn't realize it."

HENLEY: "Come off it, Vern, he kept touching his pitching fingers to the spot. What are you going to tell me next, he was trying to rub it off? No, that's it!! He's got it on him, I've seen it, he's gotta go. Bring on your reliever, Vern."

I was truly amazed. First of all, I had never witnessed a pitcher carrying a foreign substance on his person. Secondly, how the hell did Williams spot the left-handed Willis tapping his resources? Of course, Stan had pitched in the big leagues for a number of years and even had experience as a big league coach. But the question remained: How did he notice the tiny amount of pine tar? I mean, the pine tar that was on Willis' forearm was no more than the size of a quarter.

I cannot question Willis' intention here. I don't particularly agree with his code of pitching ethics. However, his idea was interesting. Willis was not trying to smear pine tar all over the ball. He was trying to create a superlative grip on the ball. In addition to helping his control, the pine tar doubled as an inducer to make the ball jump. All this seemed to be very sound thinking—until one weighs the entire idea against the consequences of getting caught. The penalty is so severe, that I wonder if the small advantage gained is worth the effort. By applying grease, saliva or any foreign substance to the ball, there is no guarantee that the pitcher will *win* or turn his opponents into a "hitless nine." A pitch delivered with "extra stuff" may even go wild, therefore creating adversity for the pitcher and his entire team.

I have to credit Williams with being a student of the game. Just handling the situation the way he did was a merit in itself. If Stan had gone the bureaucratic route, he might have jeopardized the prospect of having Willis ejected. By asking for Time, going down to tell Michael in the coach's box, then Michael hurrying down to Henley, this might have caused alarm to Willis and destroyed the ploy. Willis could use the time to rub off the tar and appear clean for the delayed inspection. The most puzzling aspect of the whole story is that Willis usually had tremendous stuff! He was the team's late-inning reliever and got more people out, with consistency, than most relievers in the league. Why was he fooling around with the black pine tar? Go figure it out.

Plate umpires are not sticklers for this rule and for good reason. They are concentrating on balls and strikes, not on the physical idiosyncrasies of the game's participants. Of course, the pitcher's movements are observed closely, but not in great depth *until* he toes the rubber. Henley's lack of perception *should not* be termed at all irresponsible. He does not have a camera lens for pupils and was not looking for trouble. In contrast, Henley handled the situation quite professionally after it was brought to his attention.

Stan Williams, if you ever examine your marketability in another field, Columbo is looking for another trenchcoat plainclothesman.

The Main Ingredients
Rule 1.09–1.10B; 6.06D; 2.00

With all the rules and stipulations that can be found in *the book*, it is apparent that none of these words have worthwhile meaning without the game revolving around the bat and ball. As odd as it may sound, there are regulations that must be adhered to in regard to the game's two most fundamental elements.

We all know that the baseball is white . . . or at least we assume that fact. Actually, they are pearly white, but only up until one hour before game time. Before the game dozens of balls are delivered (by the home team) to the umpires' dressing room. (The balls are still white.) Then the art of rubbing up the balls is performed on every last one. A substance called "Mississippi Mud" is carefully rubbed into the hide to take off the shiny gloss, and to improve the grip. This ritual turns the balls into a dirty grey color.

Pitchers are very particular when it comes to gripping the balls. Not every ball will give the pitcher's hand the exact same feeling of

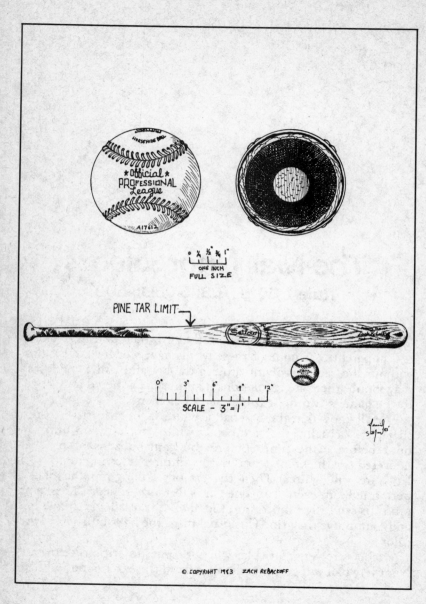

PINE TAR LIMIT

ONE INCH
FULL SIZE

SCALE - 3" = 1'

© COPYRIGHT 1983   ZACH REBACKOFF

36

The Main Ingredients
Rule 1.09–1.10 (b); 6.06 (d); 2.00

1.09 The ball shall be a sphere formed by yarn wound around a small core of cork, rubber or similar material, covered with two stripes of white horsehide or cowhide, tightly stitched together. It shall weigh not less than five nor more than 5¼ ounces avoirdupois and measure not less than nine nor more than 9¼ inches in circumference.

1.10 (b) The bat handle, for not more than 18 inches from the end, may be covered or treated with any material (including pine tar) to improve the grip. Any such material, including pine tar, which extends past the 18 inch limitation, in the umpire's judgment, shall cause the bat to be removed from the game. No such material shall improve the reaction or distance factor of the bat.

6.06 A batter is out for illegal action when—

(d) He uses or attempts to use a bat that, in the umpire's judgment, has been altered or tampered with in such a way to improve the distance factor or cause an unusual reaction on the baseball. This includes, bats that are filled, flat-surfaced, nailed, hollowed, grooved or covered with a substance such as paraffin, wax, etc.

No advancement on the bases will be allowed and any out or outs made during a play shall stand.

In addition to being called out, the player shall be ejected from the game and may be subject to additional penalties as determined by his League President.

2.00 An ILLEGALLY BATTED BALL is (1) one hit by the batter with one or both feet on the ground entirely outside the batter's box, or (2) one hit with a bat which does not conform to Rule 1.10.

comfort. If you are under the impression that all balls are the same size, you're wrong. There can be as much as ¼ inch of play in a ball's circumference.

The balls are usually made in Haiti. The height and width of the seams may vary slightly and this will prompt pitchers to ask the umpire to exchange balls. I've had pitchers ask for three or four ball exchanges on the same request. I've also gone so far as to put five balls in my mask, walk out to the mound, and ask the hurler to choose the sphere he wants. Showing him up you say? I tend to agree.

Every ball used in a professional game must be stamped with the league's name and president's signature. *Only* these balls may be used during the contest. On occasion, a delivery of balls to a particular team may become "fouled up." A completely different league's stamp is marked on the many dozens of balls. What now? The team has 40 dozen balls, but the balls have found the wrong league. In this case, the team's general manager would call the league president and explain the predicament. He would ask for permission to use these same grade balls, and permission would most likely be granted.

As you can see from rule 1.09, the baseball may weigh no less than the 5 ounces avoirdupois and no more than 5¼ ounces avoirdupois. The circumference is no less than 9 inches, no more than 9¼ inches. Thank God, I have never been part of a protest on the size, weight, or shape of a ball. I never kept a scale on hand at the ballpark.

Of course, you must have noticed that umpires examine baseballs and discard them from further game usage. Reasons? Grass stains, lopsided, nicked, scraped, shoe polish, or just plain too dirty. Each umpire has a different interpretation of the qualifications a ball must meet in order to be regarded as "fit for play." I loved examining balls, and throwing them out. Baseballs never argue when ejected.

Now, a *bat* can cause problems! A celebrated instance involved George Brett of the Kansas City Royals on July 24, 1983, at Yankee Stadium.

Catchers are well aware of each hitter's stick as they are squatted only inches from the wood. With winning taking top priority, every small advantage is taken into consideration. Even if the defensive team's protest of an illegal bat is *not upheld*, the hitter may very well have had his concentration broken. In any case, how does the plate umpire handle a situation when a batsman strolls up to the plate with a questionable bat in his hands? The umpire cannot, of course, see through the wood to detect an inserted cork or other illegal substance. Furthermore, how can he discern if a bat is one solid piece of wood? X-ray vision? It is best for the umpire to reserve any opinions or doubts he may have, until the defense requests an investigation. By waiting, the umpire has *not* looked for trouble, but is prepared to render judgment if need be. The usual objection a team may have to an illegal bat is that the lumber has pine tar more than 18 inches up from the bottom of the handle. If this be the case, the umpire may merely insist that the bat be removed from the game *before* the batter attempts to use the bat. This move will avoid the problem of the ball being hit and put into play, while runners advance. To backtrack *afterward,* and send runners back, creates havoc and hostility. Rule 6.06D stipulates calling the batter out for the infraction, as well as enforcing the ejection rule.

A good rule of thumb for the ump to follow here is to concentrate on balls and strikes. Examining bats before a case is made, will only bring on problems and ejections. Let the players enjoy their favorite bat and wait for the protest to be brought to your attention. Incidentally, I never once carried a tape measure or needed one to measure bats. Since the plate is 17 inches wide, any argument involving the length of the bat's pine tar can be solved by laying the bat across the plate and adding an inch. If you remember the George Brett case, he actually hit a 2-run homer in the top of the 9th inning to put the Royals ahead of the Yankees, 5–4. After Manager Billy Martin had argued that the bat was illegal, the plate width was used and the pine tar was found to be in excess of 18 inches. Talk about headache? Hostility? This was a perfect example.

When Brett hit his "pine tar" home run, one of the most unusual controversies to arise in many years was unfortunately uncorked at Yankee Stadium, captivating the nation for a number of weeks. Brett's homer was disallowed by the umpires and, ironically enough, became the single most controversial play of the 1983 baseball season.

On Sunday, Aug. 7, 1983, American League Umpire Nick Bremigan (one of the four umpires involved in the game) publicized (in *The New York Times*) his in-depth view of the play in question. Bremigan's summation, including relevant rule history, provides this book with an extraordinary writing effort. I could not agree more with Bremigan as his clarifying synopsis expresses true logic, diplomacy, and pinpoint understanding of the situation's complications and the extremely touchy American League position.

There is not a single word I could add to Bremigan's review. You are about to enjoy one of the best (if not the best) rule men in the world, exercising ingenious insight and logic. I thank Nick Bremigan for his permission to reprint his article.

How Baseball Became Unstuck by a Rules Dispute

By NICK BREMIGAN

To my recollection, no single regular-season incident in baseball history has captured so much attention as did that of George Brett and his pine-tarred bat. Popular sentiment was certainly on Brett's side. It rubbed the American spirit of common sense and fair play the wrong way when four umpires ruled that one of America's favorite players should be deprived of a pivotal home run in a crucial game situation.

To understand why this whole incident happened the way it did, it is necessary to consider several points of history, law and common sense.

Whenever a group of men is charged with the responsibility of producing a legal document, some imperfections are likely to result. Witness the Magna Carta, the United States Constitution and, certainly, the official playing rules of professional baseball.

None of these documents is inherently perfect or absolutely infallible.

There is no perfect rule book. The Constitution requires amendments, as well as constant interpretation from legal minds, in order to make the day-to-day business of American society operational.

The baseball rule book is also an imperfect instrument. It is constantly being amended, usually at baseball's annual winter meetings. It, too, requires constant interpretation from baseball's version of those entrusted with legal enforcement—its umpires.

Unfortunately, the parallel ends here. In the case of the Constitution, most amendments improve the overall document, at least when considered in view of the popular sentiment in effect at the time in question. In the case of the professional baseball rule book, however, most of the amendments (rule changes) have historically made the overall document more imperfect.

The reason for this is that many rules concepts are mentioned in more than one place in the rule book. The Rules Committee is empowered with formulating rule changes. When the committee sees fit to amend a rule, it often does not make certain that corresponding sections of the rule book are also amended to be made compatible with the change intended. As a result, inconsistencies and ambiguities are created, which often put one rule in diametric opposition to another, and/or put the intent and spirit of a rule in conflict with the letter of the rule.

This was the problem that confronted us around 4:45 P.M. on that muggy Sunday afternoon in Yankee Stadium and led to our ruling on the incident in question.

To understand fully how this situation developed, we have to trace the history of the rules involved to see how rule changes over the years led to the letter and the spirit of the rule being so far out of alignment.

Before 1976, all illegal bats were lumped into one category. The penalty for getting caught using one was that the batter was out and anything that resulted from his hitting the ball nullified. During the 1974 and '75 seasons, three separate incidents occurred concerning illegal bats—one involving a bat loaded with cork and two involving bats that had pine tar too far up the handle. This rash of incidents within a relatively short period of time caused the Rules Committee to decide to amend the rule in question at the 1975 winter meetings. Their intention was to create, in effect, two separate and distinct categories of illegal bats and make the penalties different for each.

The first category would include all illegally doctored bats except those treated with pine tar only. In other words, all bats that had been tampered with in such a way as to enhance the bat's distance factor and/or cause an unusual reaction of the bat surface against the surface of the ball.

These would include bats filled with lead or cork, as well as those treated with wax, paraffin or a similar substance. The penalty for using such a bat would be that the batter would be called out, lose his hit, and any runners on base would return to their original bases. In addition, the batter was to be automatically ejected from the game, as well as possibly being subjected to further discipline at the discretion of the league president.

This penalty was considered too severe to enforce for a bat that simply had pine tar more than 18 inches up the handle. The rules committee intended to keep the 18-inch limitation in effect, but the intended penalty was only that the bat be removed from the game.

A supplemental directive to umpires from the American League office made it clear that a pine-tar bat was not to be included in rule 6.06(d), which refers to doctored bats. The directive ended, however, with the statement that the 18-inch limit would still apply. This clearly removed a pine-tar bat from the penalties in rule 6.06(d)—that is, the batter is out as well as automatically ejected and possibly subjected to further discipline, but it still left intact the 18-inch limit.

Also left intact and unamended were several corresponding rules. By being left in the rule book unamended, they led to the letter and the spirit of the whole illegal bat concept being directly opposed. When confronted with Billy Martin's allegation that Brett's bat was illegal, the four of us conferred and quickly reviewed the applicable rules: One, rule 6.06(a)—"A batter is out for illegal action when he hits an illegally batted ball." Two, definition of an illegally batted ball in rule 2.00: "An illegally batted ball is . . . one hit with a bat which does not conform to rule 1.10." And three, rule 1.10, which clearly states that "The bat handle for not more than 18 inches from the end, may be covered or treated with any material, including pine tar, to improve the grip.''

Putting these three rules together, one can readily see that the letter of the law clearly indicates that there was no choice but to call Brett out and nullify his home run.

Americans' sense of honesty and fair play was understandably outraged. You will never even find an umpire who thinks that calling Brett out for such a trivial infraction was the fair, just or honest thing to have to do. No one seriously contends that the pine tar was instrumental in Brett's hitting the ball into the right-field stands.

But such is the unenviable lot of an umpire at times—caught between what the law says you have to do on the one hand, and what should be the fair, just and honest thing to do on the other hand.

This incident will probably be remembered as the one in the season of '83 on which a league president overruled his umpires.

But a careful examination of the facts involved will indicate even to the casual observer that that is not what is really happening here. What Lee MacPhail, the American League president, actually did was to rule against an ambiguous and contradictory set of rules that allowed the entire situation to develop in the first place.

MacPhail's statement said that the umpires' position was ''technically defensible.'' But once you sift through all the rhetoric and verbiage that has descended upon us in the last two weeks, the inevitable conclusion is that the umpires' decision was far more than technically defensible. Umpires are not afforded the luxury of a period of deliberation of several days, being allowed time to receive and evaluate advice and input from a myriad of sources before determining whether the spirit and the letter of the law are in accord with each other.

What we have here is a classic case of the umpires being caught in the middle, armed only with the confusing set of rules with with we are sent out each day to sit in judgment. In that light, our decision was absolutely inescapable and in full accordance with the letter of the law.

My father always taught me to look for the potential good in any rotten situation. The Brett bat incident certainly qualifies as a rotten situation for four umpires to have to be in. I suppose no one will ever write a perfect rule book. That would be about as possible as standing on the beach and trying to halt the incoming tide.

But certainly, better care should be taken by the powers in baseball to bring the rules into sharper focus and to better communicate to the umpires their intentions in effecting whatever amendments and changes they see fit to make. Some good can come out of this situation if the baseball rules committee will correct some of the countless inconsistencies and ambiguities that currently abound in the official playing rules.

Then, perhaps, we can all get back to the business at hand and to what makes the grand old game so grand indeed—a classic confrontation between a great hitter and a great pitcher being decided by the individual performances of professional athletes with the game on the line.

OFFICIALS AND OTHERS

Proper Position of Home Plate Umpire

I'll never forget the days when the Yankees were "The Baseball Dynasty" through the 1950s and early '60s. From 1949 through 1964, the Yankees won the American League pennant every year but two! I was, at that time, growing up in the Bronx. Watching Mickey Mantle was without a doubt the greatest enjoyment of my life (well, hitting a Spaldeen—a small rubber ball—three sewers was a trifle more satisfying). Dramatizing each one of "The Mick's" feats were the Yankee broadcast trio of Red Barber, Mel Allen and Phil Rizzuto. I believed everything they said. After all, who knew more then the "Voices of the Yankees."

As the years passed, I became aware of the mere mortal powers that broadcasters possessed. Also, I became more alert to their lack of knowledge about umpiring and the finer rules of the game. This is why everyone continues to ask me about the difference in strike zones for the American and National League. What difference? Both leagues utilize the same rule book! (Contrary to what former Yankee and present Yankee broadcaster Bobby Murcer

Proper Position of Home Plate Umpire

says, both leagues *do* use the same rule book.) On Aug. 19, 1983, the Yankees completed and lost the famous pine-tar game. After the televised last four outs, Murcer, opinionated and annoyed, expressed his feelings about the entire situation. He mentioned that to eliminate this and other types of interpretational controversies from recurring "both the American and National Leagues should use the same rules!" I agree with that. However, *they have been* doing so for many years. Each league *does,* however, issue an additional set of instructions to their umpires on certain ways of interpreting specific rules and other league priorities. These manuals are called "Special Instructions to Umpires."

Bobby Murcer should be applauded for his eagerness to express his opinion. However, again we are influenced by someone who appears (to the public) to be an overall baseball expert and is again misinforming the public because of his spontaneity, potential to be heard and past experience. Murcer had neglected to research the entire situation before rendering his view publicly. So now, everyone in and around New York City who heard the broadcast probably believes the leagues are operating on two different sets of rules. (Absurd!)

This brings us to what the public, in general, knows about the proper positioning for umpires. Remember, if you are not an umpire, or never had been one, you probably have obtained your previous information on the subject from TV or radio braodcasters.

I don't envy your choice of attaining information, but I cannot blame you as the umpire's position is strictly trivial to most baseball fans (until they believe we blew one against their team. "Hey, did you see the damn umpire? He had lousy position!")

In any case, up until about six years ago all umpires in the American League used the *outside* chest protector. All umpires in the National League used the *inside* protector. Let me clear up all the questions you thought were answered by your previous mentors.

Let's start with the inside protector. It is worn inside a shirt that's one size larger than normal. The protector is basically made out of the same material as the catcher's chest protector (some protectors are made with Vinyl covering). The shoulder bones are protected by a football-type pad—foam on the inside, hard plastic for the outer shell. That's it!! Now you are ready to field 95-mph fastballs off your chest with no pain. If you believe that, there is a bridge in Brooklyn that I'd like to sell you. While the protector does ease some of the shock of a foul ball, it is equally safe to say that the ball will hurt you . . . but good!

Now over there in the once more-protected American League, the umpires had it made. For one thing, the large outside protector completely covers the torso including the neck, shoulders, arms, hands and just about everything you would consider not popular with your threshold of pain. This type of protector is quite logical if you ask me. After all, there is *enough* abuse thrown our way during a game. I doubt blocking fouls would help induce perfect judgment.

Once the leagues established their particular armor, it was now a question of how to position our arbiter in coordination with his protector. Okay. American League umpires, you umpire directly in back and above the catcher, while you National Leaguers get in "the slot." The theory? Since the outside protector was large and bulky, it could not fit down in the slot (between the catcher and hitter), whereas the man utilizing the inside protector could squat in there with no problem.

My opinion? *Narrow thinking!* I know because I've tried the outside protector in the slot. From my experience (which includes utilizing both the A.L. and N.L. styles) the better position is *in the slot!* However, the better protector is the outside type. What I discovered by experimenting with the "forbidden third option" was that you see the pitch extremely well, and eliminate the chance of getting your body bruised or broken. What more could the umpire ask for?

The most commonly asked question about the leagues' different positioning of umpires is what relevancy is holds for the strike zone. Let me put your minds at ease. Both leagues have the same interpretation of the strike zone—the armpits to the knees. (Hmm, we need to examine that statement a bit later.) The only real difference is that what appears to be the strike zone in one's eyes may differ from another . . . or another . . . or another—

especially when you're viewing the pitcher from different angles (directly above or in the slot).

If you are using the outside, you are going to be sitting up higher than the inside view where you have squatted farther down and to the side. (The slot, of course, seesaws with the hitter's choice of batter's box.)

The difference in positioning results in a varying view of the low pitch. The slot man has a better view of the low pitch as his head is nearer to the ball's flight and he has no immediate obstruction under him, all the way to the catcher's glove. A good hard pitch at around knee level is a strong indication that the pitch met the requirements to be declared a strike (of course, that is, if we all agreed it had the plate as well). After all, *"the pitch was **right there**"*—right in front of the ump's eyes. The slot man's view of the inside pitch is, of course, excellent because he has positioned himself right on the corner. No one in the park can see it more clearly, except the catcher, but his opinion is a bit biased. (Asking the catcher to respond honestly and officially would be like asking a lion if he likes meat.) Whether the pitch is a strike or not, they want it to be a strike, no matter what. The slot man's principal problem is the outside corner, which is farthest away from him and partially obscured by the catcher's head and shoulder. With game experience, the umpire develops a plate width of his own and dismisses the problem of the obstruction by tuning in his built-in radar for those occasions.

Now, the A.L. umpires who utilize the outside form of protection have a complete view of both corners. His is not in a complete squat, but rather a slight knee bend which gives him the over-the-head look. This is about a foot higher than his N.L. counterparts. Here, the low pitch will have to be right on the knees for the right arm to be put up. It's not that he wouldn't like to call the borderline pitch a strike, but being so high up, he can't see the ball's last few feet of flight without bending his head (not a good idea considering a foul ball could split it open). Therefore, for years the N.L. umpires called the "low strike" more consistently then the A.L. staff, who would have equal consistency, but an inch or two higher.

49

This brings us to the "high strike." First of all, let me put to rest for good the theory of the high strike. "The book" claims the strike zone is from "the top of the knees to the armpits." If any umpire from either of the major leagues consistantly called strikes *above the belt,* he would be looking for new work. Why? Don't ask me, I only worked there. Pitches in the area from the waistband or belt to all points higher are called *balls.* Forget the book for one second. I will repeat: from the belt up, it's a ball! After my first year or two in the game I became aware of the importance of *calling the low strike* and the added importance of calling the high strike a ball. To my credit, managers and players were arguing with me less when I adjusted my zone to those guidelines.

Most baseball broadcasters know this unwritten rule because either they are ex-ballplayers or they have been around the major league game long enough to know. Oddly enough, I've never heard one actually divulge this inside info to the public. Well . . . now you have it!

This leads us to the change in the umpire's protection, which came about six or seven years ago. It was announced that all umpires in the minor leagues would have to use the inside protector and work in the slot, exclusively. All umpires in the A.L. would have the option of continuing to work with the "balloon" or switching to the inside and slot. Most A.L. umpires did change, leaving a small group of veterans clinging to their traditional protector.

Suggesting the exercise of this option was open-minded for the usually conservative umpire hierarchy. I agree with their theory . . . in part. From experience, I agree you do see the pitcher better in the slot. However, I don't see the point in getting back there only partially protected. Why not combine the outside protector with the slot position? The perfect solution! No fear of injury and the confidence of getting the best look you can. I never quite understood the risk of injury that was inflicted on the slotmen. (Incidentally, I worked in the slot for all eight of my years in the minors and suffered through the black and blue syndrome which culminated with a broken wrist in 1982. It was inevitable.)

Umpire schools emphasize the importance of keeping a straight back when *crouching*. Is this why they feel the balloon can't fit in the slot? The correct way to assume the slot position is for the umpire to have his head one head-length above the catcher's and one head-width to the side. Of course, after an umpire learns, through experience, about comfort, he will adjust his position to what feels right, and what works best for him. *The bottom line is calling the same pitches the same way consistently.* If you're going to have your low strike an inch below the kneecap, call it there every time. (Easier said then done.) The same with the other areas of the strike zone. It is physically and mentally impossible to dissect every pitch, and see it true every time.

There are distractions that arise without notice such as the batter's hands momentarily obstructing the umpire's view, or the spontaneous shift the catcher may make during the pitch which may also block your view for a split second. The most important rule the umpire should follow is to get set ahead of the pitcher's release and stay *set* the whole pitch, right into the glove, only moving his eyes, if necessary. Never move the body or the head. If the batter starts to swing, but then tries to check it, the plate umpire would be better off lending most of his concentration to the pitch location, as the swing may be appealed to the base umpires. You can't appeal the pitch! I am not suggesting the plate umpire shed one of his principal responsibilities, which is all decisions on the batter, but rahter that he place his priorities in the proper order. By focusing too much on the bat and wrist movement the umpire might conclude that an offer was not made at the ball. Fine. But now, what about the pitch? The slider might have been a strike, but a momentary loss of concentration could reverse all the good intention and work that was concentrated on the pitch.

Writing this book gives me the opportunity to voice my opinion in many areas . . . publicly. For the safety of all umpires and for the integrity of the game, I suggest that the slot position be used universally with the extra dimension of the outside protector used to secure the proper safety precautions for all umpires involved.

Base Umpire Interference
Rule 6.08D

I've got a personal experience and a humorous story for you here. In addition to the comedy, this incident triggered one of the most severe physical pains I endured in my tenure in pro ball. Getting hit by a vicious line drive has shocking results. Incredible pain.

It is only logical to assume that if a batted ball touched, grazed, or squarely hit an umpire, some compromise would need to be reached. While hockey or other sports permit the game's object to be guided or misguided as long as it remains in the arena or field of play, baseball does not want its umpires to hinder or enhance any personal achievements. I tend to agree on this point. But my question is: Why has a greater emphasis been placed on batted balls over pitched or thrown balls? I say this because according to the rules, a thrown or pitched ball that is deflected by an umpire remains alive and in play. In contrast, a batted ball upon hitting an umpire always results in a dead ball and compromise. Interesting, yes?

In 1976, I was umpiring in Greenwood, S.C. (Class A Western

Base Umpire Interference
Rule 6.08 (d)

6.08 The batter becomes a runner and is entitled to first base without liability to be put out (provided he advances to and touches first base) when—

(d) A fair ball touches an umpire or a runner on fair territory before touching a fielder.

If a fair ball touches an umpire after having passed a fielder other than the pitcher, or having touched a fielder, including the pitcher, the ball is in play.

Carolina League). The Braves were playing one of the other three teams in the league, I can't remember which one. I'd rather not make one up, so let's just leave it at that.

I do remember Gary Cooper. Coop was the fastest runner in the league. He would stretch more doubles into outs than anyone I've seen in baseball . . . period! This guy could run, but he wouldn't stop. In any case, Cooper was hitting from the left side, with a runner on first. I was positioned in the infield on the first base side of second. I was 25 years old at the time, and considered myself as agile as any umpire in the game. I used to dare myself to get in as close as I could to attain the best possible angle on pick-off attempts at first. I don't remember standing too close on this particular evening. I'd say I was about 90 to 100 feet from home plate, when Cooper lined one that had "screaming liner at your crotch" written all over it. I really couldn't believe the shock that came over me when I realized that this was it! I leaped and cringed as the hooking low liner cracked an excruciating blow right under my kneecap on the inner side of my left leg. Embarrassment could not penetrate the severe pain that was spreading through my entire body with the center of throbbing activity located at the leg. I stayed down and fought the first few minutes of agony from the ground. My partner, trainers and players stood around staring at my grimaced face, until the pain subsided enough for me to stand. Only a steady throbbing remained. I felt like quitting for the night. I had a perfect excuse; however, I felt I couldn't leave only one authorized umpire to call the remainder of the game.

Suddenly, I remembered "Where's Cooper?" The other runner?? Had I called "Time?" It then occurred to me that all was under control and the delay would terminate as soon as I was able to continue.

The heavy throbbing continued, and the swelling gradually took form, but I couldn't keep from wondering if I had done something wrong, or if the contact point of the line drive had met the requirements to be ruled a dead ball. The position of the infield umpire dictates the call. If the umpire is behind the infielders, another ruling would be in effect. The ball would continue to be alive and in play, taking into consideration that no other infielder had a chance to make a play on the ball.

For many years, the N.L. and A.L. umpires differed in positioning the umpires down the first and third base lines as well as positioning the second base umpire with a runner on first. On the lines, both leagues had the umpire stand about 10 or 15 feet behind the first baseman. No matter how close or deep he decided to play, this gave the player plenty of room to dive and not interfere with the umpire on shots right down the line. However, one league had its umpires straddle the line, the other wanted both feet in foul territory. One day, a few years ago, they decided to make the stances uniform and had everyone stand with both feet in foul territory. (This arose from umpires actually taking fair balls on the muscle—and preventing a sure double). Now they can block foul balls that have no significance other than a possible souvenir for a lucky front-row fan.

There is no omen or moral to this story other than the black and white facts. Maybe I should say black and blue, as my entire leg from thigh to foot was indeed black and blue with a tint of orange for four weeks! This little bit of experience was quite helpful in determining my position as I moved up to the AA and AAA levels where they really hit hard line drives . . . consistently. My advice: Play deep and move your ass, man!

Home Plate Umpire's Interference

Rule 5.09 (B)

It's truly amazing how much trouble one umpire can run into just following the game. You can image the verbal abuse that comes his way if he actually interferes physically with a team's chance for an out or a hit.

The plate umpire is out of just about everyone's way, including the catcher's . . . until his throwing comes into play. It's only normal that the catcher rear back and whip that arm for all the mustard he can get on it. The umpire is no more than a couple of feet away, at the most. Fortunately, the catcher's stride toward his objective will greatly decrease the chances of contact with the man in blue as it is only natural to step toward the target when throwing.

When a runner reaches base, a throw behind him or to catch him stealing is obviously feasible. Now, our umpire must take into consideration the catcher's throwing mechanics which include leg shifting, uncoiling, rearing back to throw, and follow through, in addition to all decisions on the batter and the pitch. Catchers are, by and large, husky men who can make their strength felt at will,

Home Plate Umpire's Interference
Rule 5.09 (b)

5.09 The ball becomes dead and runners advance one base, or return to their bases, without liability to be put out when—

(b) The plate umpire interferes with the catcher's throw; runners may not advance.

NOTE: The interference shall be disregarded if the catcher's throw retires the runner.

especially to an unsuspecting umpire. If he uppercuts the umpire's jawbone with his shoulder, it is safe to say the enchanting voices of the unsympathetic manager and catcher will be screaming that he blew their chances of retiring the runner.

Folks, there are times to exercise diplomacy, and there are times to lose your temper. If you were choking umpire, which course of action would you choose? a) *Gee fellows, I'm awfully sorry about this; how can I make it up to you?* or b) *Hey, listen you——, you can kiss my——! What do you have, a crystall ball in the dugout? No one knows if he'd have been out or safe!* There are rules for plays like this, and that's what we go by. The runner returns, the game resumes, and find me a mouthpiece!

Rulings on plays not specifically mentioned in the Rules
Rule 9.01C

I really don't know where to begin telling you about my most embarrassing moment on the professional circuit. Actually, there is a logical explanation for my insane ruling. However, I don't believe it would go over with the managers, players, and an *(almost)* national TV audience.

Let's begin with some relevant background. Marshall Brant (now with the Oakland Athletics organization) is one of the most intelligent baseball players I have run into. He is a very tall, handome, free-swinging first baseman, who had started his baseball career with the New York Mets organization and moved on to the Yankee chain around 1981. Marshall was a bona fide home run threat every time he stepped up to the plate. However, he was equally proficient at striking out. Marshall and I always enjoyed our tour of duty at first base together, capitalizing on the premise that few people could actually tell we were carrying on a conversation while he was on defense. It was usually a fun night—until, of course, Marshall thought I blew one that cost him or his team, let

59

alone if I called a play that cost him a precious point or two in his struggling batting average. He always knew how to turn into a S.O.B. like the rest of them. In any case, I liked Marshall and I guess I always will.

Now, the story. The place—Columbus, Ohio. The year—1981. The beautiful confines of Franklin County Stadium presented an extra touch of excitement today because for the first time a national TV cable network was airing the second game of the scheduled doubleheader. Why?? The major league players baseball strike was about one week young, and American was craving baseball on TV.

The young Entertainment and Sports Programming Network (ESPN) chose this stadium as its showcase for its first telecast to be seen all across the country. It was an exciting day for everyone at the ballpark. I remember that day for many reasons, among them that *only* the second game would be televised. While working first base in the opening contest, I could't help wondering how I would react to calling balls and strikes for game No. 2. I was ecstatic!

With the first game deadlocked at 1–1, the Tidewater Tides were out on the field, in the bottom of the fourth. Brant had reached first somehow, and was taking his lead with one out. Ronald McDonald, the Tides first baseman, was holding Brant on closely. I was stationed in the normal pick-off position a few feet from the bag in foul territory. The hitter, Rick Stenholm, lined a fierce one-hopper right at McDonald, who scooped it out of the dirt in pure self-defense, if nothing more.

Under normal circumstances, the first baseman, in this situation, steps on first, then fires to second, to get the reverse double play. The shortstop covering must bear in mind that the play at second is a tag play, not a force. The force was removed once the first baseman had stepped on first to retire the batter-runner. Realistically, Brandt could retreat to first if he wanted. When Marshall saw that the hard smash was trapped my McDonald, he instinctively assumed that Mac would go for the reverse D.P. So did I!

As it turned out, Ron's first play was to fire to second to force

**Rulings on plays not specifically mentioned in the Rules
Rule 9.01 (c)**

9.01 (c) Each umpire has authority to rule on any point not specifically covered in these rules.

Brant, anticipating plenty of time to receive the relay, to double up Stenholm. I moved into my infield position to wait for the return toss and call the back end safe or out.

The only problem here was that Marshall, anticipating Ron's plan, ran a few steps toward second, then reversed his field, and headed back to first. Why? Because he figured he would be returning to first at around the same moment McDonald would be throwing to second. Brant realized he'd be a dead duck at second, because the ball was hit so sharply, and he was by now means a speedster. Brant had no idea that he had, for all reasonable purposes, been put out at second by Ron's first play. Confusing? Hey, if you think that is confusing, you should have seen my confused face when the relay back to first arrived, and McDonald was awaiting the throw so he could put the quick tag on the head-first sliding Brant! Brant beat the play by a millimeter so naturally I called him "Safe!"

The dust cleared, and there was Marshall standing with two feet on the base wiping off his dirty uniform. I called time and silently praised myself for being on top of the play. McDonald, Brant and I were now regrouping our thoughts, when the three of us started frowning at each other. Jesus Christ, I couldn't believe it. I wondered, where the hell is Stenholm?

By this time, my partner, John Hirschbeck, was starting to walk up from home plate. Tides manager Jack Aker was right behind him. I never felt so foolish on a baseball field. I had been taken in by the confusing moment, completely disregarded the back end of the D.P., and now the Tides would have to pay for my confusion. (To my credit, I can at least say that McDonald didn't appear too sharp either. But how the hell was I going to explain this to Aker?) More importantly, how was I going to correct the error?? What would be correct? Was Stenholm out or safe? I didn't know! Was McDonald's foot on the bag when he received the relay? Again, I didn't know. It is irrelevant if he tried to put out Brant again. If his foot was on the bag, and the ball was there ahead of Stenholm, then it should have been a double play.

First things first. Brant, who looks like a damn monument to me by now, has got to go. He's out. Stenholm, of whose whereabouts I had absolutely no idea (and still to this day he has not been called safe or out), has to change places with Marshall. That should fix things up, right? Would you be eager to tell that to Aker? I wasn't, but I did.

I started, "Jack, I know I screwed this one up, bad. However, I had enough good common sense to realize my mistake, and rectify it the best I can. Brant will be out, Stenholm safe!"

Jack calmly and diplomatically replied, "Zach, if you want to truly rectify your call, you have got to call it a D.P.—because Stenholm *was* out at first!".

"Come on Jack, how can I be certain Mac was on the bag? I wasn't looking, as I was focused on the slide play."

"Zach, he was on the bag, I saw it!".

Jack gave me a foot in the door. Now I retaliated by saying "Jack, how can you say that when you're down in the dugout some 200 feet from the play? I'm not even positive that *the ball was there in time!* I have no alternative but to die with this call, and hope you understand my predicament."

Jack concluded by stating, "Zach, I don't agree with this outcome, but I accept it". With that he turned and as calmly as he arrived, headed back to his dugout, defeated.

Can you believe that? I still have trouble making people believe I was a victim of circumstances. Sure, I lacked total concentration on the play, however, considering the circumstances can you blame me? What's worse, could you imagine me trying to explain this one to a large TV audience? That would have been the backbreaker. The Brooklyn Bridge wouldn't have been high enough for me.

Failure to Comply with Ejection Rule
Rule 4.15F

Where does the official draw the line? I've asked myself that question scores of times. The umpire is undoubtedly "The Enforcer." However, every umpire must keep in mind never to overadministrate his authority. He also must maintain his logic when it comes to enforcing severe penalties. The rule book dictates many apparent cut and dry rulings, but fails to mention the severe repercussions of being "too technical." Umpires' skin needs to be tough, durable and pliable. His ears need to be stuffed with plaster in order for him to fully control the game. This might sound unusual, but more respect will be given to an umpire when the team knows they can blow off steam that is actually *spontaneous hot air.*

Taking these outbursts, gestures, and game pressure into consideration, our umpire must also draw the line on vulgarity, obscene gestures and flagrant disrespect. Permitting team personnel to rant and rave is not exactly what the Rules Committee has in mind.

Failure to Comply with Ejection Rule
Rule 4.15 (f)

4.15 A game may be forfeited to the opposing team when a team—

(f) Fails to obey within a reasonable time the umpire's order for removal of a player from the game.

When a player, or manager or trainer for that matter, directs obscene language personally toward an umpire, it is unquestionably grounds for immediate ejection. There is no if, and, or buts about it! I would say at least 75 percent of the ejections I declared in my eight years were rebutted by the culprits claiming "I didn't say anything" or "I didn't do anything." Odd how often our ears can play tricks on us. Nevertheless, once an ejection is announced, "that's all she wrote!" Period. They gotta go, no reprieves. Actually, some of the stories in thier own defense do sound legitimate, but of course they're clutching a false hope.

Now, there are occasions that dictate special handling. When an ejected player begins to create a delay of the game by not leaving the field or dugout, the game should not be resumed until he does.

The "watch tactic" should not be employed unless no other alternative is possible. Of course, some veteran umpires may have long-running rapports with their players, and the tactic could be used as a ploy to scare them into believing the worst. Options? 60 seconds to leave without a police escort, 60 seconds to leave with a police escort, or 60 seconds to leave or the game is forfeited! By no means should the umpire tolerate this brand of totally inconsiderate, disrespectful behavior. All the team backing in the world could not ethically support the players' refusal to leave. Should our umpire decide to indeed forfeit the game, he would certainly be within his jurisdiction to rule in this drastic manner. After all, if one player is allowed to make a farce of the game, what will prevent the rest from following in his footsteps?

In 1976, Lee Elia (recently the Chicago Cubs field manager) was managing the Class A Spartanburg Phillies in Spartanburg, S.C. In those days, Elia and I did not see eye to eye . . . on anything. He gave me a hard time every ballgame I worked for him, and I ended up ejecting Lee three times that season.

One of those ejections brought out the devilish antics of a young stubborn schoolboy in Elia. He refused to leave and as I stood by home plate waiting. Elia sat, with arms folded, directly on home plate!

In only my second year of pro ball I was apprehensive as to what course of action to pursue. I was positive that I would not just stand there and have Elia amuse the large crowd at my expense. Realizing that the hot sun beating down was making me thirsty, I decided that this was a perfect time to walk over to the visitor's dugout and refresh myself with a good, ice cold glass of water.

Now, to Elia's surprise he was sitting on home plate with no one to embarrass but himself. He was, ironically, outmaneuvered by my clever diplomacy. He must have thought I was going to plead with him to leave. Everyone, including myself, put one foot up on the dugout steps and peered out at Lee, who was just basking in the sun. Elia looked foolish, and he soon realized it. He had no other option but to stand up, dust off his backside, and leave the field muttering under his breath.

In my opinion that particular case was handled perfectly, but could have ultimately resulted in a forfeit. To this day I applaud myself for having the restraint and composure to outfox Elia at his own shenanigans. For argument's sake, what if he continued to sit on the plate? I believe I would have pulled the watch on him. I am, however, thoroughly pleased I didn't have to find out.

Photographer's Interference
Rule 3.15

I am the first one to admit that photographers are important to baseball. Hell, I wanted my picture in the newspaper more than anyone. I remember times when I actually turned my head so "my good side" would be staring at me in the morning paper. After a while, you know where the photographers are, and what kind of shots they're aiming for. And you thought umpires were colorless!

So, in effect, I loved having the camera buffs out there—the more the merrier. However, having them on the field brought out one quirk in me. I hated them getting *too* close to the action. If I could spot a cameraman out of my peripheral vision, then he was simply to close. I would always halt the action, and signal for them to clear out or move back. I did this for two reasons.

First and foremost, it was to protect them from being beaned or losing an eye. The second reason was to eliminate the chance of the interference they could inflict on the game by their presence. Even though the rule stipulates that no penalty is invoked for unintentional interference, it still would create enormous problems. I

Photographer's Interference
Rule 3.15

3.15 No person shall be allowed on the playing field during a game except players and coaches in uniform, managers, news photographers authroized by the home team, umpires, officers of the law in uniform and watchmen or other employees of the home club. In case of unintentioanl interference with play by any person herein authorized to be on the playing field (except members of the offensive team participating in the game, or a coach in the coach's box, or an umpire) the ball is alive and in play. If the interference is intentional, the ball shall be dead at the moment of the interference and the umpire shall impose such penalties as in his opinion will nullify the act of interference.

could think of 200 players who would love to scream their lungs out at me for not keeping the camera snoops out of play. Umpires, in general, do not need additional problems. I've worked with umpires before who actually permitted a camera crew (two or three people) to monitor the game from 30 feet directly behind home plate. From my position in the infield, I would call "Time" and bring it to the home plate umpire's attention. I would ask myself, how could he *not* be aware they are back there?? Was it that the umpire wanted the local coverage, or was it that he simply did not have the nerve to instruct the media? It would not be a "pretty picture" if a passed ball or a foul ball lodged in the cameraman's neck! How would that appear? For starters, I can tell you that if the ump claims he "didn't see them," then he's not doing his job properly. In addition, if the base umpires overlook the situation, they deserve an equal amount of the blame.

In most major league stadiums, photographers have the convenience of their own *working box*. They are safely tucked in near the dugouts and can click away to their heart's content. However, in the days of yesteryear, photographers could be spotted squatting or kneeling as near to the action as on the deck circle—and sometimes closer! Lenses were not as powerful as today's models, and the game became accustomed to the photographers' presence. With today's technology, of course, everything has changed. Ballparks do have sectioned-off areas for cameramen, and the only contact they make with the players is holding them upright when they invade the photographers' area for a diving catch of a foul pop-up.

In minor league and amateur parks across the country, these luxuries are not consistently evident. Umpires must be conscious of those preoccupied cameramen who are constantly looking for the perfect angle to snap the perfect picture.

This situation has never been more evident than in Santo Domingo in the Dominican Republic. These guys seemed to be coming out from under the foul lines. They're everywhere! Down the line, in the dugout, behind you, over there, over here . . . They remind you of gnats. Great guys but, man, could they monopolize foul territory! I remember one night I was watching a game on TV.

(I had the night off, so what else was there to do at 8 p.m.?). A screaming line drive whizzed down the third base line, (and before the TV camera could focus on the ball's flight), took down an unsuspecting photographer, holding his temple. Evidently he had his camera up to his eyes, and was not able to react before the line drive was upon him. He was standing about a foot off the foul line, a few feet behind the third base umpire. This Dominican was carried off on a stretcher! He was hurt very badly. This casualty could have been prevented had the third base umpire been a man of just a few words like "Hey, get back out of play." That does not mean in *foul territory*. Foul territory is not *out of play*. The cameramen must station themselves so if they need to move quickly they will avoid any interference with a ball or fielder. The problem became so prominent in Santo Domingo, that two small booths were constructed for the opening of the 1981 Winter League season. The booths were situated alongside the end of the dugouts which placed the photographers about 150 feet from home plate. They absolutely hated it! At that time I was chief umpire for the entire league and the poor guys pleaded with me to let them creep out of their cage and again attain the angles they once so proudly owned. "Take it up with the league president," I advised them. "No," they argued. "You are the chief, you can give the word!" I loved their tact, but they couldn't budge my strict observance of the new law. (I really did not see the point of having 20 men stuffed in a cubbyhole, but I certainly couldn't take them scrambling around during the game). Besides, I couldn't overrule "El Presidente." I am a softy at heart, so I did speak to "El Presidente" and we made some allowances.

In closing, my principal objection to these creative specialists being too close was for safety reasons, whether it be another country, or the good ol' U.S. of A. I cannot stand by and see anyone injured by a hard ball. A baseball can be a lethal weapon, and if not properly protected against, may lead to excruciating pain and serious injury—not to mention death! You photographers bear this in mind the next time you sense your creativity overstepping your logic.

Batter Refuses to Take His Position in the Batter's Box
Rule 6.02C

Umpires, in general, are aware of giving players the benefit of the doubt in many situations. What I mean by that is, if a touchy situation does come up, our officials need to remain cool and consider the course of action that will result in the least amount of disturbance.

However, there is one situation that is a perfect time for going by the book, without the constant reminder of the end result. If that hitter does not get in the box to hit, after warning, I vote to make it tough on him . . . and temporarily easy for myself. Plate umpires are under the constant strain of calling balls and strikes consistently throughout the ballgame. *Only* an intentional walk breaks up the intense pressure of following extremely difficult pitches. Plate umpires are constantly being made the goat by hitters, claiming the inept umpire is to blame for adding a strike to the count. Umpires are trained, and then continue to train themselves, to maintain their composure when a team or player is inflicting embarrassment upon them.

Batter Refuses to Take His Position in the Batter's Box
Rule 6.02 (c)

6.02 (c) If the batter refuses to take his position in the batter's box during his time at bat, the umpire shall order the pitcher to pitch, and shall call "Strike" on each such pitch. The batter may take his proper position after any such pitch, and the regular ball and strike count shall continue, but if he does not take his proper position before three strikes are called, he shall be declared out.

There does come a time when the umpire can finally ease the pressure for the pitcher, catcher, hitter and himself. If that batter continues to ignore the warning and refuses to take up his position in the box, the ump should not plead with him to do so. Just have the pitcher pitch! No matter where the pitch lands, it's called a strike. You watch how fast our ignorant batsman gets in there.

Now don't get me wrong here, folks. I am not suggesting that this rule be enforced every time the batter steps out to question the call—only in cases where the batter's behavior is in blatant disregard to the umpire's fair warning. The hitter does not have a leg to stand on.

I have been inches away from making this call on a number of occasions. Each time, the hitter realized he was in jeopardy of grave consequences and resumed his stance. I would have been happy to experience this moment just once in my career. I guess I can't really complain, as handling this situation without playing all my cards was an accomplishment to be proud of.

Different Official Decisions on One Play

Rule 9.04C

From the first day I entered umpire school until my active career ended, one of the strongest "don'ts" impressed upon me was making a double call, especially when the calls were "safe" and "out!"

Bear in mind there are different ways to work each set of field mechanics. This unusual situation is particularly likely when the crew is engaged in a play that demands rotation. One might ask why the umpires would not *see* each other maneuvering for coverage. That is a logical question, and one that is logically explained.

When umpiring, the ultimate objective is to keep your eyes on the ball—*always!* The ball will, in turn, lead you or turn you to the play. No ball, no play!

The umpires who are moving with the play are continuously focusing on the ball as well, with occasional glances to cover runners circling the bases. Therefore, each umpire is not fully concentrating on where the others are, but rather expects them to

Different Official Decisions on One Play
Rule 9.04 (c)

9.04 (c) If different decisions should be made on one play by different umpires, the umpire-in-chief shall call all the umpires into consultation, with no manager or player present. After consultation, the umpire-in-chief (unless another umpire may have been designated by the league president) shall determine which decision shall prevail, based on which umpire was in best position and which decision was most likely correct. Play shall proceed as if only the final decision had been made.

be covering their own responsibilities according to the system in use.

Another unwritten rule says that *once* an umpire goes *out* (to the outfield for further coverage) he is technically supposed to *stay out,* and leave the bases or his base to the rest of the rotating crew. The crew remaining knows he is out, and reverts to a system they have planned for working with one less official than usual. When and if the umpire comes back to position himself for a call, this is exactly the time you look for confusion.

For example: Let's say there's a runner on first. The hitter lofts a fly ball down the left field line. Our speedy third base umpire needs to run down the line as far as he can, *stop,* and determine all factors including fair, foul, catch, no catch, spectator interference, etc. The home plate umpire now moves in to cover third, in the event the runner tries to go from first to third. Each umpire on the field is glancing at the runners. They are not necessarily looking for their partners. In this instance, the third base umpire may have counted on his partners' adaptability. In any case, combined with the crowd noise, it's a favorite to create havoc. Here comes the play, the guy slides... and it's close! There were our umpires sizing it up, stride for stride and then finally concluding. Both umpires were of course prepared to call it... and did! (It's possible that out of the corner of their eyes they noticed each other, but their priority was to *see* the play, and call it. Neither was sure the other would call it. Additionally, both feel responsible!) They couldn't possibly stop, look at each other and hesitate. That's not very professional.

Actually, with both teams screaming bloody murder, the crew chief gathers his forces for a conference. The consultation is based on who actually had the better look, all things considered. With good judgment prevailing, the outcome will be favorable to the true act. Any decision will undoubtedly cause one team to argue ...again!

Spectator Interference
Rule 3.16

Spectators have always played a considerable part in creating or diminishing team momentum. Although fans do not participate physically in the feats that are accomplished *on the field*, their presence is felt. A roaring crowd can catalyze a rally or stir up enough electricity in the air so that you can almost feel a monumental feat in the making.

Fans, however, do get carried away. They occasionally let their selfishness overstep their integrity. Sometimes fans place emphasis on capturing a souvenir without realizing they are actually *altering* the outcome of the play or the game. Bearing this in mind, our crew of umpires must be aware of the field's dimensions and the seating arrangement of the stadium. Most minor league ballparks do not have the extra seating capacity the bleachers provide. This eliminates any spectator interference on balls that are hit and stay in fair territory.

In contrast, almost all major league stadiums *are* equipped with outfield bleachers. There always exists a threat of fans reaching over to snare long fly balls or balls approaching the outfield fences on a bounce. Base umpires are continuously leaving their infield responsibilities to the remaining umpires to more closely judge traps and fan interference. I have seen umpires *miss* sighting a darting arm because of the timing and camouflage involved in this particular situation.

Picture this: The ball is arcing down near the fence. The shirtsleeve crowd is preparing to fight like hell for the potential home run as the outfielder gets set for his best leap in a last-ditch effort to snare the long drive. Fans are not allowed to reach over the imaginary line of the top of the fence, because they might interfere with a ball still in flight within the confines of the playing field.

For the base umpire to rule expertly on this play, he would need to be on the same vertical plane as the fence to see if the oustretched arm of the fan has protruded onto the field or not. If the umpire could attain this position, he could witness the exact contact point, in addition to being sure if the outfielder had an opportunity to make the catch or not.

Unfortunately, base umpires cannot outrun a batted ball from their starting point in the infield. Room for error in judgment is foreseeable in this situation . . . and understandable. The chance of error on this call is much more limited in All-Star, Playoff and World Series competition, as six umpires are assigned to the games. Each umpire is assigned to a foul line, which puts him in a more strategic location to handle decisions on long fly balls.

In addition to seeing the play clearly, and assuming interference was ruled, he must also rule on the final outcome of the play, including the award of bases. Many people are under the impression that spectator interference immediately induces a call of "ground-rule double" from the officials. This is definitely not the case, however. Many times the batter and runners are awarded two bases from the time of the pitch only because, in the umpire's judgment, had there been no interference, the offense would have reached *only* those bases. Bounding balls that do eventually

338

©COPYRIGHT 1983 ZACH PEBACHOFF

Spectator Interference
Rule 3.16

3.16 When there is spectator interference with any thrown or batted ball, the ball shall be dead at the moment of interference and the umpire shall impose such penalties as in his opinion will nullify the act of interference.

APPROVED RULING: If spectator interference clearly prevents a fielder from catching a fly ball, the umpire shall declare the batter out.

There is a difference between a ball which has been thrown or batted into the stands, touching a spectator thereby being out of play even though it rebounds onto the field and a spectator going onto the field or reaching over, under or through a barrier and touching a ball in play or touching or otherwise interfering with a player. In the latter case it is clearly intentional and shall be dealt with as intentional interference as in Rule 3.15. Batter and runners shall be placed where in the umpire's judgment they would have been had the interference not occurred.

No interference shall be allowed when a fielder reaches over a fence, railing, rope or into a stand to catch a ball. He does so at his own risk. However, should a spectator reach out on the playing field side of the fence, railing or rope, and plainly prevent the fielder from catching the ball, then the batsman should be called out for the spectator's interference.

bounce up into the stands are, of course, groundrule doubles.

Fans occupying outfield bleachers brings to my mind an interesting experience I had in Santiago, Dominican Republic. The cheap seats were always packed for the big games, and the Latin fans would sit on the edge of the bleachers and dangle their legs over onto the field side. As I scanned the outfield, all I could see was a row of legs and shoes from one foul pole to the other. I was totally confused on what to do. How did this practice ever get started here, I wondered—because it was actually allowed! When I requested that the public address announcer publicly request those spectators to remove their bodies from the fences, it was as if I had not asked them anything. They didn't budge . . . not one of them!

I confronted the home team manager, Ozzie Virgil, one of the first Dominicans to play in the major leagues. Ozzie made me aware of the custom.

"Zach, this is Santiago in the D.R., not the States. These people have been doing that for 30 years! You can't change it, so don't worry about it.

"But", I retorted, "It's the biggest lock they'll interfere with an outfielder. You can clearly see that, can't you?"

Ozzie explained, "Yes, it's happened before, but it's *no problem*. Just advise the rest of the umpires to call what they feel would be appropriate to nullify any interference and we'll go from there."

I was surprised, to say the least. This is a professional league with a high level of competition. Many major leaguers and minor leaguers from the States compete on these teams during the winter months. Ten Americans are on each of the six teams in the league. How could everyone overlook this problem with such ease? I'll tell you how: because they didn't have the responsitility to rule on the eventuality. I decided not to create a scene, but made both managers aware that their arguments would not be heard or tolerated should such an interference transpire.

With all due respect to spectators, I find their compelling need to touch a live ball inconsiderate to the game, its players, the umpires and the entire crowd on hand. Fans should be cautious not to let their personal motives interfere with the natural course of events taking place during a ballgame. Put yourself on the other side of the fence. Everyone who is an avid baseball fan would love to be there. However, the game only uses nine *professionals* at a time.

Team Owners on Bench
Rule 3.17

Team owners are becoming more and more involved with the personnel actually placed in the club's lineup. Field managers have the authority to create lineups and make substitutions at will. However, they are dealing with the priorities of the owners more than the game has been used to. The press and media have publicized this personal side to the point of creating personality conflicts between managers and owners. A perfect example of a widely publicized, long-running difference of opinions belongs to the New York Yankees, specifically "The Boss," George Steinbrenner and feisty ex-Yankee manager, Billy Martin.

Steinbrenner makes no bones about who is running the show, but consistently makes changes that cause the media and fans some skepticism. One day, he clearly grants his manager all field personnel decisions, and the next day he publicly indicates who is in or out of the lineup. Conflicting stories tend to crop up, which prompts the team to make statements to fill in the missing information. In the past, reports have indicated that "The Boss"

Team Owners on Bench
Rule 3.17

3.17 Players and substitutes of both teams shall confine themselves to their team's benches unless actually participating in the play or preparing to enter the game, or coaching at first or third base. No one except players, substitutes, managers, coaches, trainers and bat boys shall occupy a bench during a game.

PENALTY: For violation the umpire may, after warning, remove the offender from the field.

has *phoned* his manager *during a game* to offer his own input on the plan of attack.

The Yankees are not the only team that has encountered this problem. In view of the fact that the Yankees are the most celebrated team in sports history, they are subject to a high level of media scrutiny. The Yankees and Steinbrenner, as a rule, are inclined to make their opinions public and, therefore, are in danger of being quoted and misquoted by the press. George and Billy are not inhibited celebrities, and can generate publicity like no other duo.

This leads us to the possibility of a club executive wanting to get in on the field aciton. After all, *their* money is invested in *their* team, so why shouldn't *they* be able to view the game from the vantage point of *their* choice? By conversing with the field manager during the game, spontaneous evaluation and scrutiny can be exercised at the moment of truth. Their conversation would not interfere with the actual play of the game. So again, the question repeats itself. Why not let the executives occupy a seat on the bench? They *are* paying everyone's salary!

The rule forbidding any club executive from sitting on the bench does have logic, however. Starting at the top, the umpires have enough problems to cope with *without* having to be confronted verbally by the team brass. Even men who carry with them a maximum level of class are vulnerable to loss of control and could become an annoyance. In addition, the added pressure the owner presents to his players by being in close contact during the contest would make even his most confident and prolific players inhibited and could cause unnatural errors.

Front office people should refrain from entering the dugout during a game. If and when they find themselves compelled to *bend* the rules, it is mandatory for the umpires to remind them of the stipulation and ask for their removal. The situation calls for *any* of the umpires to make the observation and alert the crew chief to the problem. The crew chief should, diplomatically and sincerely, quote the rule (if necessary), and do it as promptly as possible.

In accordance with this rule, it is equally important to make sure that photographers, members of the grounds crew and suspended players abide by this rule, as well. To be honest with you, I don't see why the dugout seat is so alluring (other than rubbing elbows with the stars); the dugout is the worst seat in the house for perspective. In any case, the bench is to be occupied only by players, substitutes, trainers, coaches, bat boys and the manager. *Everyone* must be dressed in team uniform. I wonder, how *did* Connie Mack get away with that?

By the umpiring crew not observing, or claiming not to notice the infraction, they indicate they are not willing or able to handle adversity. An umpire claiming "he didn't want to rock the boat" is overlooking the rules and not administering his duties properly. If one is hesitant to enforce his authority, when he *knows* he is within his jurisdiction to eliminate a possible distrubance, he cannot make me a believer in his competency. Of course, it is possible that by handling the situation head on, it could cause an argument right at the outset. Usually however, the league would not hesitate to back the officials 100 percent.

Violent Bench Disapproval
Rule 4.08

There is no umpire who has worked in organized ball or professional baseball who has not heard he has "rabbit ears." My first
experience with this phrase brought a great deal of embarrassment
to me. I have always been blessed with large ears, yet in my
opinion they are not even close to resembling rabbit ears. In any
case, I was, on this day, addressed as "Keep your head out of the
dugout, rabbit ears!"

Now, how was a green, skinny umpire, who was barely coping
with the problem of calling balls and strikes to know that rabbit
ears referred to an umpire who has got his head and ears tuned in
on bench jockeying. I simply adjudged the remark as a personal
insult about my physical makeup. I approached this irate dugout
of Class A players and asked "Who's got something to say about
my ears?". Every player in the dugout screamed, "I do", in
unison. I was speechless, to say the least. I looked the young pros
up and down from one side of the dugout to the other and when I
finished the scan I could do little more than burst out laughing—
as did the entire dugout!

Violent Bench Disapproval
Rule 4.08

4.08 When the occupants of a player's bench show violent disapproval of an umpire's decision, the umpire shall first give warning that such disapproval shall cease. If such action continues—

PENALTY: The umpire shall order the offenders from the bench to the club house. If he is unable to detect the offender, or offenders, he may clear the bench of all substitute players. The manager of the offending team shall have the privilege of recalling to the playing field only those players needed for substitution in the game.

When the good laugh was over, I judged one player to be the team spokesman and asked him, "Why are you guys hassling be because I have little-bigger-than-average size ears? They are not even that big!" Another burst of laugher erupted and I found myself again laughing with them . . . at myself. (You readers must be wondering what was going on out on the field during this delay. No problem. Fans love to see heated arguments like this one.)

That situation was handled with incredible ease . . . and luck! A good number of bench jockeying situations end up in player or players being ejected. Varying circumstances prompt violent bench disapproval toward an umpire. Obviously, the prerequisite is for a call to go against the team. It matters little if the umpire's call is correct or not—only that they *think* you're wrong. An enraged dugout is a serious matter for the officials to contend with, and needs to be handled properly and firmly. It is only occasionally that a problem of this dimension can be solved by improvising with humor, as in the case I explained at the beginning of this chapter. Each umpire on the crew must establish a pattern of his own in regard to how he conducts business on the field and how he applies his authority. Every man has his own boiling point. Dugouts are normally a considerable distance away from home plate, making it difficult for the umpire to localize verbal harrassment. It is even more difficult to distinguish voices. Remember, 20 to 25 men are in there, with a few of them camouflaging the real offenders.

After a warning, if the constant chatter is not brought to a halt, the umpire has no choice but to exert his authority, and put a stop to it. By ejecting one of the loudmoths or chasing *all* the substitutes to the clubhouse, the umpire has remained within his rights in enforcing the rule. The official must maintain his dignity and make the team aware that he will not tolerate flagrant abuse.

In dealing with this problem on occasion (notice I wrote "on occasion;" I would not be comfortable writing this book if I had been constantly defending my calls to entire teams), officials have their own personal method of handling this ego-deflating situation. One must continue to keep his composure, and be alert to the possibility of actually lowering oneself to *their* level. A loss of control will create problems of such magnitude, that they can cause a permanent personality conflict between the entire team and that particular umpire. However, umpires are aware that when dealing with vulgarities, they must maintain a high level of tolerance, thus ensuring the umpire's objectivity for the remainder of the contest and future. Working while holding a grudge is an unsurmountable burden to overcome.

Therefore, a long, serious look through the bars of the mask can be as effective as a bench clearing. Umpires must be totally prepared to back up their words. Once they issue warning, they must be ready to take the initiative and do what they know will, inevitably, result in a game delay, ejection and a long written report to the league president. In addition to their immediate problems, league presidents, in general, do not appreciate having to resolve major field eruptions. As a result of the field demonstration, the league office will be receiving conflicting reports on the course of events. The president will have to make some kind of statement to all parties involved, and at the same time pay close attention to the rule book and reporting umpire. With this situation in mind, it is a lot simpler to rule negatively over one person rather than over an entire team. So, I ask you, who do you think that will be?

The overall situation requires much thought by the umpire. How does one handle this dilemma maturely and with integrity? There is only one answer to that one. An old adage is appropriate here and it starts by one stranger asking another, "Excuse me, how do you get to Carnegie Hall?" The answer: "Practice, man, practice!"

Coach Employed Tactics
Rule 4.06 A (3); 7.09 J

There is one old adage that never ceases to amaze me with its accuracy and that is, "you learn something new every day." It is, of course, a matter of opinion if this phrase is absolutely correct, but generally speaking, it's true. I can honestly admit that right now, I am learning something, or at the very least becoming a trifle confused about what I once believed certain regarding the baseball rules.

I have inserted both rule 4.06A(3) and 7.09J in this excerpt to share my mini-dilemma with you. Both rules have something in common: The two clearly penalize the coach for trying to create illusions for the defense.

The illustration here clearly shows the third base coach employing tactics to try to make the pitcher balk. This problem could be solved by enforcing rule 4.06A(3). In addition to nullifying a balk, if made, the coach is additionally ejected from the game. I agree with that. In my opinion, however, there are more serious crimes committed on the diamond that are not penalized by ejection. I

Coach Employed Tactics
Rule 4.06 (a) (3); 7.09 (j)

4.06 (a) No manager, player, substitute, coach, trainer or batboy shall at any time, whether from the bench, the coach's box or on the playing field, or elsewhere—

(3) Call "Time," or employ any other word phrase or commit any act while the ball is alive and in play for the obvious purpose of trying to make the pitcher commit balk.

PENALTY: The offender shall be removed from the game and shall leave the playing field, and, if a balk is made, it shall be nullified.

7.09 It is interference by a batter or a runner when—

(j) With a runner on third base, the base coach leaves his box and acts in any manner to draw a throw by a fielder;

PENALTY FOR INTERFERENCE: The runner is out and the ball is dead.

am not about to state them or get too deeply involved at this moment.

Now, in reference to rule 7.09J, it specifically directs its attention to the problem created *"for the fielders"* by our tricky coach. The penalty for this is okay. But how come no ejection? Isn't the coach's intention here as severe or more so than trying to cause a balk? In both cases the coach is trying to steal a run!

Before writing about each rule, I thoroughly examined and dissected the rule in question. That is when I realized the difference in penalties in regard to rules 7.09J and 4.06A(3). I think it is inconsistent not to enforce the ejection penalty in both cases. The coach has no business doubling as a trickster. He is responsible for relaying the manager's signals and advising runners of baserunning and scoring opportunities. I disagree with the lack of continuity in the rules which cover his spontaneous self-indulgence.

Nevertheless, the problem for our umpire is that he must be always ready for the unexpected (who would expect the coach to resort to such trickery). As I have stated previously, and as also quoted in the rule book, "umpires should keep their eyes everlastingly on the ball." In following this rule, their eyes would be fixed on the pitcher who, at the moment, has control of the ball and is preparing to pitch. From experience, I can assure you that even with your eyes on the hurler, peripheral vision allows you to pick up quick movements within a wide range. Both the third base and home plate umpires would be distracted enough by the coach to see the play and act accordingly.

Ironically, both rules 4.06A(3) and 7.09J were enforced by N.L. umpire Bruce Froemming on Sunday, Aug. 24, 1983, at Shea Stadium in New York. It was the first time Froemming enforced this rule in his 13 years as a major league umpire.

According to the New York *Daily News'* account of the play, the Met's Keith Hernandez was on third, with Bobby Valentine in the third base coach's box. Rookie Darryl Strawberry was at the plate, with two outs in the first inning.

With Chicago Cub starter Rich Bordi toeing the pitcher's rubber, Hernandez danced off third, feigning a break for the plate. Right behind him was Valentine clearly intending to confuse the pitcher by also dancing and feigning a break for the plate. Bordi stepped off the rubber, and Valentine requested that Froemming call a balk. Instead, Valentine received a warning from Froemming. I cannot locate the word *warning* in either rule.

Two pitches later, the same act was put on by Hernandez and Valentine and Froemming threw the book at them. He called Hernandez out and dismissed Valentine for the entire afternoon. These two decisions prompted me to dissect these rules very closely.

After serious examination, I am prepared to argue that if the *Daily News* account of the events and quotes are correct, Froemming interpreted the rules incorrectly.

Froemming explained to the press that Valentine was trying to make the pitcher balk. He stated that the penalty for that is that the coach is removed from the game, under rule 7.09J. Now, in reviewing rule 7.09J, there is not a word about ejecting the coach and more importantly the rule is directed at the coach's antics when trying to draw a throw from *a fielder.* In my opinion, rule 7.09J should not have even been brought into the controversy. Rule 4.06A(3) includes enough ammunition to justify ejection of both Hernandez and Valentine, but does not stipulate calling the runner *out!*

In bringing this play into its proper perspective, Valentine should have been ejected for employing tactics to draw a balk by the pitcher. This is quite clear under rule 4.06A(3). Hernandez should have been ejected as well, if he indeed was making the same movements for the same reason. Again rule 4.06A(3) justifies that precise ruling. According to the rule, however, Hernandez should not have been called out! (Of course, if a balk were committed, it would be nullified because of the unsportsmanlike inducement.) Hernandez would have had to act in quite an unorthodox manner to draw a penalty from Froemming. Merely dancing around near third base is not, in itself, reason to believe he was maneuvering with unsportsmanlike intent. I do not question Froemming here, as his judgment must prevail.

In getting my facts absolutely correct I spoke by telephone with the *Daily News'* writer, Fred Kerber. Kerber reinforced my theory by stating that Froemming (after the game in the umpire's dressing room) did cite both rules in making his decision.

Bruce Froemming, whom I have never met, has established himself as one of the top umpires in the National League. As shown by this example, it is possible for even one of the best to be confused when interpreting a rarely enforced rule. Possibly, a small conference between the game's four umpires may have brought a deeper insight and understanding to Froemming before he declared his intentions. It is entirely possible that one of the other umpires had a clearer understanding of both rules, and would inform the entire crew of his interpretation. It's rare that the umpires would stop the game and consult the rule book in the confines of their locker room and emerge with the proper call. However, as this case clearly indicates, a short rules check would have been the proper tactic.

As a result of writing about this particular play, I am now totally aware of the precise wording that covers these two similar situations. I will now remember that the coach is ejected in one case and not ejected in the other.

Therefore, even though I was under a false impression and do not agree with the inconsistency of the rules, I must admit I relearned something I had been taught nine years ago. You never know, eh?

DEFENSIVE PLAY

Pitcher

Slipped Pitch
Rule 8.01 D

In eight years of professional umpiring I've only witnessed a pitch slip out of a pitcher's hand once or twice. But I do remember the details of one particular incident.

On a picturesque baseball night in Toledo, Ohio, I was working first base. My partner, John Hirschbeck, was calling balls and strikes... and *slips!* (Incidentally, John Hirschbeck is one of the best young umpires to come out of the minor leagues in recent years, and is as strong and competent an umpire as I have ever worked with.) With no outs, no runners on base, and the count 2–1 (2 balls, 1 strike) on the batter, the pitcher's next delivery does indeed slip out of his pitching hand, and trickles to a stop some 15 feet in front of home plate, just the way it's illustrated here.

I'd been chatting with the Toledo first baseman, Kelly Snider, on and off during this "at bat," but fully recognized the "slip" and mechanically omitted the pitch from the actual ball and strike count in my own mind.

Kelly Snider turns to me and questions, "What's that?" I tell

Slipped Pitch
Rule 8.01 (d)

8.01 (d) If the pitcher makes an illegal pitch with the bases unoccupied, it shall be call a ball unless the batter reaches first base on a hit, an error, a base on balls, a hit batter or otherwise.

A ball which slips out of a pitcher's hand and crosses the foul line shall be called a ball; otherwise it will be called no pitch. This would be a balk with men on base.

him the rule, basically, and he's content with my explanation. About three seconds elapse and he quickly turns to me again and says, "I thought you said it was no pitch." I reiterated. Kelly points out, "So how come he called it a ball? Look at the scoreboard!"

Sure as I'm in Toledo, Ohio, the scoreboard reads 3–1. I called "Time" immediately and started down the first base line to question John on the validity of the scoreboard. Already out there protesting the call was Toledo's manager, Cal Ermer. John waved Cal away to confer with me privately and I could tell from John's face he was slightly embarrassed. When we met face to face we both wished we could burst out laughing, but circumstances prevented any frolicking.

Partially stunned by his momentary lapse John admitted, "It's no pitch, right Zach?"

"You got it, Toyota!"

"Now what?"

"Now nothing. Go tell him and everyone else it's no pitch. There's not going to be any argument, because nobody in the ballpark knows the rule except me. . . . Kelly Snider, and now you!"

There are times when reversing the call is not only logical, but intelligent as well. Umpires are out there to get the call right. Pride has its merit, but admitting to a momentary lack of concentration takes a man of integrity.

Pitcher, in Windup Position, Runs Off the Rubber
Rule 8.01 A, (1), (2), (3)

The rule which I am about to explain has been argued, at length, among many umpires. Not only does the situation call for careful scrutiny by the umpire, but a complete knowledge and understanding of the exact rule, as well.

As you can see from the illustration, the runner on third has broken for home. A steal of home plate is the most exciting play in baseball. It is also one of the most pressured situations for the participants. There is little or no room for error by the five integral people involved in this drama.

The cast includes, in order of appearance, the runner, pitcher, batter, catcher, and of course, ultimately the home plate umpire. Each one of these people has a specific obligation and objective in carrying out his duties. The first person to indicate the steal is on is the theft-thinking runner. He has clocked the pitcher's windup procedure, and has made a mental plan of how to pull off the theft. He waits for the exact moment to break, trying to induce the pitcher to commit a balk or release a wild pitch.

At the same time, the pitcher will need to decide which course of defensive action to pursue on his own. He has two options. The first is to disengage the rubber, by stepping off backwards with his pivot foot first, thereby becoming an infielder. He can now run or throw at will. By choosing this route, the jittery hurler eliminates the chance of balking. A balk would bring home the run no matter how many times the catcher tags him.

His second option is to continue through his normal windup and deliver his pitch to the batter, hoping the ball and tag will be ahead of the speedy thief.

This now brings us to the home plate area. The betting line is 10–1 that the batter is aware of the play, and will try to create some type of legal adversity for the catcher to aid the attempt by his teammate. He must be careful *not* to linger or create an illegal distraction. This would result in interference and make the entire effort worthless. The runner would be called out!

In the meantime, the catcher must be ready for anything. Naturally, his first priority is to catch the pitched or thrown ball. He must then make every effort to control the ball quickly while blocking the plate from the steamrolling runner. (A quick spin back in time brings to mind the infamous Jackie Robinson theft of home in the 1955 World Series. I've seen that play several times on tape. I try never to question the judgment of another umpire, however, if Robinson was *safe*, then I'm a pilot for Eastern Airlines! Yogi Berra, the Yankee catcher, was waiting, having a cup of coffee, *before* Robinson even went into his slide! I will admit that this type of play *does not* give the umpire reasonable time or the opportunity to move for position and a good angle. The best advice here is that if the ball beats the runner to the plate, call him *out*. Boy, was Yogi mad!)

In any event, the final decision on the entire play rests on the shoulders and judgment of the home plate umpire—and it doesn't start or end with a simple ruling on the ultimate tag. The umpire does not have the freedom to make a contribution to the play, then wait for the result.

First of all, he needs to carefully observe the pitcher's preliminary movements. Did he adhere to the pitching rules? Did he

Pitcher, in Windup Position, Runs Off the Rubber
Rule 8.01 (a) (1) (2) (3)

8.01 (a) The Windup Position. The pitcher shall stand facing the batter, his entire pivot foot on, or in front of and touching and not off the end of the pitcher's plate, and the other foot free. From this position any natural movement associated with his delivery of the ball to the batter commits him to the pitch without interruption or alteration. He shall not raise either foot from the ground, except that in his actual delivery of the ball to the batter, he may take one step backward, and one step forward with his free foot.

When a pitcher holds the ball with both hands in front of his body, with his entire pivot foot on, or in front of touching but not off the end of the pitcher's plate, and his other foot free, he will be considered in the Windup Position.

The pitcher may have one foot, not the pivot foot, off the rubber and any distance he may desire back of a line which is an extension to the back edge of the pitcher's plate, but not at either side of the pitcher's plate.

With his "free" foot the pitcher may take one step backward and one step forward, but under no circumstances, to either side, that is to either the first base or third base side of the pitcher's rubber.

102

If a pitcher holds the ball with both hands in front of his body, with his entire pivot foot on or in front of and touching but not off the end of the pitcher's plate, and his other foot free, he will be considered in a windup position.

From this position he may:
(1) deliver the ball to the batter, or
(2) step and throw to a base in an attempt to pick-off a runner, or
(3) disengage the rubber (if he does he must drop his hands to his sides).

In disengaging the rubber the pitcher must step off with his pivot foot and not his free foot first.

He may not go into a set or stretch position—if he does it is a balk.

quick pitch? Disengage properly? Did the batter cause flagrant interference to the catcher? What about the pitch—ball or strike? Now, *bang,* call the play!

From the appearance of the illustration and the rule interpretation, it certainly appears that the pitcher met the necessary requirements to stay within the pitching rules and eliminate the call of a balk. However, I must point out one small gray area of the rule. As you can see, the pitcher did disengage the rubber, but did he do so legally? He must disengage by stepping off the rubber *backwards,* moving his pivot foot first in that direction. The Rules Committee has erred slightly in not clearly mentioning *backwards.* Rule 8.01E does specifically mention the word *backwards,* stating that by the pitcher doing so he would now be considered an infielder and able to perform *out* of the confines of the pitching rules.

This tricky backstep takes place in the same time it takes to bat an eyelash and could be missed completely if the umpire is not prepared to look for it in advance. The funny thing about the *step* is that when we (the umpires) have failed to recognize it, it seems the whole offensive team has seen the infraction and is screaming "balk." Now that's embarrassing!

Pitcher Defacing the Ball
Rule 8.02A(5)

A particular episode associated with this rule has an ironic outcome. The play took place in Santo Domingo in the Dominican Republic in the winter of 1980. The truth of the matter never surfaced until July, 1983, in New York City. I am positive it was the truth because the perpetrator (Gerald Hannahs) revealed it to me 2½ years later on Broadway and 49th Street.

During the winters of 1979 and 1980 Gerald Hannahs was a star pitcher for the Licey Tigres. The Tigres (that's Tigers in Spanish) were the strongest team in the entire Caribbean in 1979–80. They proved it by winning the Caribbean World Series, whose participants were the champions of all the winter leagues, which include Puerto Rico, Mexico, Venezuela and, of course, the D.R. Hannahs was virtually unhittable that winter and went 12–0 for the season. Hannahs had pitched in the Montreal and Los Angeles organizations prior to his remarkable winter campaign.

The next fall he again returned to the Tigres and was expected to take up where he had left off the year before. Gerald pitched

© 1983 COPYRIGHT ZACH REBACKOFF

Pitcher Defacing the Ball
Rule 8.02 (a) (5)

8.02 The pitcher shall not—
(a) (5) deface the ball in any manner;

PENALTY: For violation of any part of this rule 8.02 (a) (2 to 6) the umpire shall:

(a) Call the pitch a ball, warn the pitcher and have announced on the public address system the reason for the action.

(b) In the case of a second offense by the same pitcher in the same game, the pitcher shall be disqualified from the game.

(c) If a play follows the violation called by the umpire, the manager of the offense may advise the plate umpire that he elects to accept the play. Such election shall be made immediately at the end of the play. However, if the batter reaches first base on a hit, an error, a base on balls, a hit batsman, or otherwise, and no other runner is put out before advancing at least one base, the play shall proceed without reference to the violation.

(d) Even though the offense elects to take the play, the violation shall be recognized and the penalties in (a) and (b) will still be in effect.

(e) The umpire shall be sole judge on whether any portion of this rule has been violated.

well that season, but was not the phenom of the year before. One beautiful Caribbean evening with over 20,000 screaming "fanaticos" packed into Quisqueya Stadium, Hannahs was turning the ball over remarkably well from that junk-balling left arm of his. The pitches did not raise suspicion in my mind. However, there was one thing that persisted in making my wonder. By examining the present game ball and a couple of balls in my "ball bag" I noticed unusual scrapings across the cowhide. I noticed it again after yet another inning—an inning in which Hannahs had just finished inducing the opponents into making three easy outs. The ball that Hannahs just finished using again had the unusual scrapings! I decided that when Hannahs took to the mound in his next inning of work, I would investigate his integrity.

Never before in my professional career had I taken on this type of investigation. I wasn't exactly sure how I would proceed, but there is a first time for everything. When Gerald walked out to the mound, I approached him and said, "Hey, Gerald, I've been collecting these defaced balls throughout these first few innings." (I was carefully analyzing Gerald's reaction, looking to see if he would crack under scrutiny.)

There was no reaction from Hannahs other than, "So, what are you telling me about it for?"

"Because," I explained, "it's my job to locate the offender and you're the prime suspect!"

Hannahs replied convincingly, "Well, go ahead and check me if you want," and he proceeded to spread open his arms, opening himself up for a closer look into his proclaimed innocence. At this very moment the Licey manager, Del Crandall, arrived on the mound to make his own investigation of what was happening to his star pitcher. I contemplated frisking Gerald, but decided that without the other team insisting on a search, I had already made it a bigger issue than I had originally intended. Hannahs seemed more than willing to go along, and that in itself was reassuring. I concluded the investigation and left Hannahs to warm up.

Our story continues on July 9, 1983, the place, 49th Street & Broadway, in New York. I had just seconds before walked out of seeing the new movie *Psycho II* when who comes strolling down the avenue but Mr. Hannahs. Surprised and happy to see one of the fellow Jewish boys from the diamond, I uttered, "Hello, Gerry Hannahs!"

"Hey Zach, what the hell are you doing in New York City?"

"You got it wrong, Gerry, I live here. What the hell are *you* doing drawling people to death with your presence here in the Apple?" (Gerry owned a genuine Southern drawl). After the initial greetings were completed, we walked along the avenue, recalling names and places we had become so accustomed to a few years ago. We stopped, and with my arms draped over a parking meter, I asked Gerry "Hey, remember the night in Santo Domingo when I came out to check you? Remember the balls had funny marks on them? What's the deal, were you doing it?"

Without hesitation or looking for a lawyer, Gerry simply replied, "Yes."

"So, how were you doing it," I asked. "With your fingernails?"

"Nope, Zach. Under the extended flap of my belt I had attached a small piece of sandpaper. With the extra leather that was left over from the buckling area I covered the sandpaper. When I got the ball back from the catcher I would appear to be pulling up my trousers and would move the leather back, scrape ball, then reposition the flap securely under the belt loop."

Hannahs was smiling now, but not wider than my own grin. "Look at that," I said to myself. "I knew something was up."

We finished up our informative conversation and said our goodbyes. While walking away, I couldn't keep from wondering what would have transpired had I detected the foreign substance. Ejection, of course. What about Hannahs' loyal 20,000? Man, that would have been a sight to see, a police escort in the makings. In any case, he put it over on me. How do you like that? And I thought I had a trace of Columbo in my blood.

Ball Lodges in Umpire's or Catcher's Mask
Rule 5.09G

This particular coincidence immediately brings to mind this question: Why would face masks be constructed to allow a baseball to stick in between the bars? If I were manufacturing face masks I would take every precaution to eliminate the slightest chance of that happening.

For example, a new Wilson wire mask has an eye level opening of 1 ¾ inches. An official baseball's diameter is approximately 2 ¾ inches which, of course, leaves 1 inch of safety. Logic dictates the ball can't squeeze in. The two other spaces above and below eye level are 2 inches wide at their maximum width, so again it appears safe, right? Right! So why was this rule inserted in the book? Because of the hypothetical possibility. Let me explain.

Years ago, before technical improvements were made in the process of manufacturing equipment, catcher's and umpire's masks (they are one and the same) were properly named "bar masks." The mask was constructed by using lateral bars to allow maximum horizontal, vertical and peripheral vision to its user, and

Ball Lodges in Umpire's or Catcher's Mask
Rule 5.09 (g)

5.09 The ball becomes dead and runners advance one base, or return to their bases, without liability to be put out, when—

(g) A pitched ball lodges in the umpire's or catcher's mask or paraphernalia, and remains out of play, runners advance one base;

If a foul tip hits the umpire and is caught by a fielder on the rebound, the ball is "dead" and the batsman cannot be called out. The same shall apply where such foul tip lodges in the umpire's mask or other paraphernalia.

If a third strike (not a foul tip) passes the catcher and hits an umpire, the ball is in play. If such ball rebounds and is caught by a fielder before it touches the ground, the batsman is not out on such a catch, but the ball remains in play and the batsman may be retired at first base, or touched with the ball for the out.

at the same time to provide protection. It had no vertical bars or wires for support. Needless to say, the mask lacked the strength to continuously withstand foul balls hit against hard-throwing pitchers. Enter the "wire mask." This type of mask allows perfect vision (except for occasionally obstructed views when peering straight down), but most importantly just about guarantees that the ball will not stick or go through.

The wire mask has upper and lower shock absorbing pads shaped to fit snugly around the user's forehead and chin. It is quite safe if he faces the oncoming pitch directly without lowering or lifting his head. Not facing the pitch could very well result in serious injury. The umpire should by no means depart from these guidelines.

Nevertheless, it is *still* possible for the ball to stick in a wire mask. Why? Because umpires (and catchers) receive numerous foul balls off the mask. The constant impact of foul balls eventually takes its toll on the mask and, in time, dents or reshapes the formation of its wired front. Some umpires gloat over the "notches" on their mask, although most others take their vulnerability in stride, periodically evaluating their viewing space to determine if a new mask is in order.

When a mask has reached its life expectancy, I recommend a new one for a number of reasons. Number 1 is that your vision is slightly obstructed if your wire is bent every which way. You can never tell when you might need that small bit of extra peripheral vision. Secondly, after too many foul balls, the wire tends to weaken and it is possible that with the impact of just one more, the wire may crack and send a broken edge inside at the eyes or face. That is an ugly possibility, don't you agree?

Returning to the case at hand, of course, it is entirely possible for the catcher to miscalculate the direction of the pitch and miss the ball completely or have it deflect off his mitt.

Tell me about it. Juan Espino missed a pitch completely in August of 1982 that was a 90-mph fastball that fractured my wrist. Espino jumped out, expecting a pitch out, and Lynn McGlothen aimed for the strike zone. That pitch zoomed straight at my crotch. I couldn't believe the moment! I had my hands draped in front of my crotch, so naturally I took it on the wrist. Oddly enough, with the bases loaded and a 2–2 count on the batter, strike 3 was the proper call. I could have strangled Espino, but with no opportunity to do so, my only rebuttal was to call the pitch "a ball." Without intending to pun, it was one of my weakest calls. I sobbingly crawled to the visitor's dugout, screaming in pain the whole time. All the players expressed deep concern by suggesting I smile for the TV camera, which was now focused on my face. Baseball is a lot of fun—until it hurts!

There is one technicality regarding the rule that I would like to bring out at this time. As you can clearly read in the second paragraph of rule 5.09G, the words "foul tip" are used. Twice, as a matter of fact. You see it? Stop here and read it carefully. Now if you will check this book's glossary you will see that a foul tip is defined as a pitched ball that is tipped by the bat and goes sharp and direct to the catcher's hand or glove. Correct? Then why has the term "foul tip" been inserted here in 5.09G?

The Rules Committee is making the same assumption that is made continuously by fans, managers, players, broadcasters, and just about everyone else. No matter how slightly the bat grazes a pitched ball, if it does not go sharply and directly to the catcher's hand or glove it is simply a foul ball! (How can the word "foul tip" be used in this paragraph of rule 5.09G when the ball never was controlled by the catcher? It is absolutely impossible for a "foul tip" to lodge anywhere except in the catcher's glove or hand!) A large percentage of baseball fans consider a tipped ball a foul tip. If it were a foul tip, the catcher would be controlling it in his hand or glove. I hope this is clear to all my readers, as I have been waiting to clarify this for a long time.

Catcher's Balk
Rule 8.05L

Every umpire who has worked in pro ball has (on occasion) visualized the fantasy of "catcher's strangulation." You will not find this term listed in this book's glossary (or any glossary, for that matter), or in any "special instructions to umpires." However, believe me, it has crossed *my* mind numerous times—and the fantasy always has me doing the strangling.

The catcher—our nine-inning working companion—two of them, no less! It's like having three plate umpires assigned to the same contest. However, the job is made substantially easier if each duo works together (until a close one goes against a catcher; then, even the Pope himself couldn't be convincing). The catcher and umpire will try to work together on giving a "good shot" (that is, a good view of the pitch) and maintaining a pleasant working atmosphere throughout the game.

However, there are times when the ump must put his foot down and establish his authority, even on a technicality. The intentional pass is a free ride for the players involved, including the umpire.

**Catcher's Balk
Rule 8.05 (1)**

8.05 If there is a runner, or runners, it is a balk when—

(1) The pitcher, while giving an intentional base on balls, pitches when the catcher is not in the catcher's box.

Not much pitch preparation or finesse is necessary to decide the four easy tosses that are 4 to 5 feet outside of the strike zone. (I've actually witnessed N.L. umpires Bruce Froemming and Ed Montague with their masks dangling from their hands, waiting for the boring ritual to be completed.)

But, you never really know in this game. Johnny Bench was made to believe he was being intentionally passed in a World Series, and the relief ace blew a third strike right by him. As you can see by the illustration, the umpire is watching the catcher flagrantly and effortlessly commit a rule infraction. Everyone in the ball park can see it as well. How does a plate umpire overlook this predicament? I mean, are we to let the whole ballpark suspect we are sleeping back there, or that we just don't care?

A common practice by catchers is to slide out from the catcher's box simultaneously to the pitcher's release, or at least within that same time proximity. The benefit of the doubt will usually be given to the catcher. However, taking up residence outside his confines while the pitcher is still in his windup, is overdoing it a little. After all, I've seen a wild pitch advance a runner during an intentional base on balls. By leaving his box too soon, the catcher is obviously trying to eliminate that chance. Our clever receiver will have to do some fast talking to his manager explaining why he blew the team's strategy by *now* having the runner or runners advance as a result of the balk. The intentional walk was originally issued either to create a force situation or pitch around a strong hitter to get to the weak stick behind him. In all of the games I've worked, witnessed in person, or have seen on TV, I have never seen this rule enforced.

Catcher's Interference
Rule 6.08C

Catcher's interference was actually the first difficult call I had to make, (and which confused me; there have been many others since.) It is unusual that in my first plate appearance in an organized game, I was confronted with this. In your first game, it is confusing to know where to stand, let alone deal with interference calls.

I will *now* never forget what steps to take in ruling on this play, as umpires differ in their interpretations of exactly how and when the call should be made. This particular incident brought one of the all-time great umpires, Al Barlick, to argue the point with a present major league umpire, John McSherry, whom I consider one of the top men in blue in both major leagues.

An interesting part of the training and evaluations implemented at umpire school is to have the student-umpires work major league intrasquad games. These major league teams open their spring training camps at approximately the same time the umpire school is in operation. These warmup games are a valuable tool in evaluating the student's talent. If any serious miscues were made by the nervous and inexperienced umps, it was considered no problem, as the game was merely a team workout. In 1975 I was assigned to work home plate for the Philadelphia Phillies, with manager Danny Ozark at the helm. To be perfectly frank, I was nervous!

Sitting directly above the home plate area, in an observation deck, was Umpire Development Supervisor Barney Deary; N.L. umpire and school instructor John McSherry and Al Barlick. They were to scruitinize every aspect of *my* game. When I realized the position the ''Big Three' had taken, I was even more nervous, however in control of the situation I might have been.

In the very first inning, a batter swung at a good pitch, and caught the back of the catcher's glove, although still maintaining enough leverage and control to loft a soft pop-up which appeared to be heading over the first baseman's head. The batter quickly turned to me and cried ''Hey, I hit his glove!'' I, in turn, emphatically replied ''Interference, first base!'' Note: my declaration was made before the ball dropped in, and also before the batter reached first base. The batter proceeded to move gingerly toward the bag, as I put up my hands and called ''Time.'' I was so damned nervous, I thought I was dreaming. I felt reassured when nobody said a word, the hitter took first by my award and the game resumed. I figured I must have got it right.

That evening, all six umpires who had participated by rotation during the six-inning workout, were called to a meeting with McSherry to go over the day's events and evaluate our work. When John got to me, I could tell from his opening remark that he was in disagreement with the ruling I had made regarding the interference. He told me that the call sparked a mini-argument between Barlick and himself. Barlick claimed I was perfectly correct, and handled the situation like a bona fide professional. He reasoned that by my calling the play approximately at the same time the hitter complained, I would eliminate the opposition from claiming he influenced my decision. That could incite an argument about who is actually calling the game. McSherry disagreed with Barlick, and the timing of my decision, insisting that interference

Catcher's Interference
Rule 6.08 (c)

6.08 The batter becomes a runner and is entitled to first base without liability to be put out (provided he advances to and touches first base) when—

(c) The catcher or any fielder interferes with him. If a play follows the interference, the manager of the offense may advise the plate umpire that he elects to decline the interference penalty and accept the play. Such election shall be made immediately at the end of the play. However, if the batter reaches first base on a hit, an error, a base on balls, a hit batsman, or otherwise, and all other runners advance at least one base, the play proceeds without reference to the interference.

If catcher's interference is called with a play in progress the umpire will allow the play to continue because the manager may elect to take the play. If the batter-runner missed first base, or a runner misses his next base, he shall be considered as having reached the base, as stated in Note of Rule 7.04 (d).

should have been called when it was clear that no other runners would reach their next bases safely and that the batter-runner would not reach first safely.

After experiencing this situation countless times thereafter, I would come to rule on this play by combining both McSherry's and Barlick's interpretation. How? When and if a batter does indeed smack the glove with his bat, I would immediately *announce* "Interference", and then continue to wait for the outcome of the ball in play. Then, and only then, would I call "Time" and award such bases as would nullify the act of interference. This way, everyone knows you were aware of the backlash, but waited to rule by evaluating the next set of circumstances. In addition, waiting allows you a little more time to analyze the situation, and get your ruling in order by the time the play is completed. A familiar baseball saying comes to mind here, one I always found amusing, as well as authoritative: "It ain't *nothing* 'til I call it."

Illegal Use of the Mask
Rule 7.05D

"Illegal use of the mask." Sounds like a 15-yard penalty. It's truly amazing how many times I *thought* I might have to rule on this play. To my surprise, not one of these situations ever resulted in the mask coming into play.

As I have mentioned occasionally throughout this book, I've often pondered how or why certain rules come to be inserted in the official rules. This particular case only confused me for a few short moments. I'm sure there *were* instances that prompted the catcher to use the mask to corral a wide throw. As managers and players found loopholes in the rules, the Rules Committee closed them.

Other than stopping errant throws, catchers may use the appearance of the mask to gain a possible advantage. Catchers need to be good actors (not to mention liars) on occasion. For example, when a runner is trying to score, and the catcher is aware that the throw will be a fraction too late, he may very well have a good idea by appearing to look disappointed that the throw will be late, and there is no chance to retire the runner. By standing at home plate, his catchers mitt held down and the *mask dangling freely* from his throwing hand, the overall message conveyed by his body language can be misleading to the steamrolling base runner. If the runner goes for the ploy, he will slow up and coast into home,

**Illegal Use of the Mask
Rule 7.05 (d)**

7.05 Each runner including the batter-runner may, without liability to be put out, advance—

(d) Two bases, if a fielder deliberatley touches a thrown ball with his cap, mask or any part of his uniform detached from its proper place on his person. The ball is in play.

believing there is no play on him. The catcher may now come out of his trance, and block the plate with a new outlook on the play's outcome. In doing so, the catcher may very well forget that he is still clinging to the mask, and when the ball and runner arrive simultaneously, the mask may make contact with the ball. If the ball does pop loose momentarily, intentional or unintentional use of the mask warrants the enforcement of the rule.

Taking this one step further, a catcher who is just learning to catch on a Little League or amateur level may not be aware of this rule, and decide to be creative by snaring or blocking the ball with his new acquisition. Not a bad thought . . . shows imagination. Why didn't I try *that* one at umpire school? (Refer to *The Cap Catch*, pg. 195.)

Ball Lodges in Catcher's Protector
Rule 5.09G

Is it possible for a pitched or thrown ball to lodge inside the catcher's protector? It's not easy, but it is feasible.

Some catchers allow their chest protectors to fit loosely on their chest and around their shoulders. I've always felt that the tighter the protector was worn, the more protective and cushioning it would be. Incidentally, the material used to compose this protector is not what you would call a safeguard against broken bones or chest bruises. While I agree that the protector needs to be pliable for mobility, I feel the protector delivers insufficient protection.

In any case, a ball could conceivably enter through the neck opening or up under the bottom. Considering these possibilities, the catcher could create the illusion of a momentary loss of the ball's whereabouts, providing the rule had been kept as it was several years ago. At that time, a ball caught up under the catcher's protector would be a live ball. I assume the rule was reversed to conform with the umpire in this case—to eliminate the possibility of the catcher sticking the ball inside his protector on purpose. By doing this, the catcher could appear to be searching for the errant ball, but actually be waiting for a base runner to try to advance. Then, pulling the ball free, the catcher would have an easy play on the unsuspecting runner.

**Ball Lodges in Catcher's Protector
Rule 5.09 (g)**

5.09 The ball becomes dead and runners advance one base, or return to their bases, without liability to be put out, when—

(g) A pitched ball lodges in the umpire's or catcher's mask or paraphernalia, and remains out of play, runners advance one base.

Inasmuch as the old rule would work against a tricky catcher, I would be willing to bet that catchers would not execute this ploy. I say this because of the pressure that a game situation presents. Catchers do not have the time to entertain pipe dreams when under fire. It is difficult enough to execute the basics of the game, let alone improvise with longshots. I nod my head in agreement with the rules committee for exercising good judgment by improving this particular rule. By doing so, they have alleviated an added burden for the umpires in addition to maintaining the game's fair play and integrity.

124

Catcher's Obstruction
Rule 7.06B Note

On the subject of obstruction, I would like to share an experience with you that I was fortunate to have witnessed. Before I do that, let me provide some relevant information.

Catchers have been getting away with little tricks since the game originated. After all, when the play is at the plate, anything goes ... including blocking, hooking, neighborhood tags (tagging someone in the *neighborhood* of the base or body) and even so much as appearing to control loose balls after collisions. Let's not forget that the steamrolling runner is capable of his own tactics, such as, but not limited to, bulldozing and kicking the ball loose. Therefore, the umpire must be a trifle more lenient when calling plays at home plate. The "dish" is the ultimate fortress for maximum defense, while the offense strives to break through and claim a run. To say *anything goes* would really not be absolutely correct, but may the feistiest man win.

In view of this slight leniency, it would be safe to assume that most umpires working home plate are not looking for obstruction to occur at the plate. A normal pattern for the umpire on this play would be to first clear the area (if time allows) of any bat or mask, then prepare to position himself at an overall good angle to see the

**Catcher's Obstruction
Rule 7.06 (b) Note**

7.06 (b)

NOTE: The catcher, without the ball in his possession, has no right to block the pathway of the runner attempting to score. The base line belongs to the runner and the catcher should be there only when he is fielding a ball or when he already has the ball in his hand.

play. Almost 60 percent of the plays at the plate result in a swipe tag. In this instance, the catcher must corral the ball, then come back, lunge, and tag the runner, who is doing all he can to evade his touch by hook sliding.

So, as you can see, it is clearly unusual for the catcher or umpire to be thinking *obstruction*. In nine pro seasons, I have seen this rarity only once—and I was a spectator!

126

In 1975 I was driving through Clinton, Iowa, where I stopped and took in a Midwest League contest. I took a seat some 10 to 12 rows up behind the plate, yet looking down the third base line. I could see perfectly with plenty of scope to spare. If I was on ground level, like the umpire, I could not achieve the wide range of sight. I can empathize with our umpire for not catching the act.

As I saw it, the runner had rounded third and was barreling home, apparently able to beat any close play. It also appeared that the throw from left field would be some 6 to 8 feet wide of the plate, and would pull the catcher that distance away from his established position blocking home plate. (He could have stayed there, but would have had no chance to stop the ball.) The only way to possibly cut off the pending score would be for our deceiving catcher to *appear* to maintain his position, but somehow still stretch to his left for the off-line relay and still block the plate, then come right back and apply the tag. Only problem here was that he blocked the runner first, moved to get the wide throw, *then* came back and made the tag. He did not *need* to be in both places to catch the ball!

Realize now that the umpire is naturally preparing for a swipe tag, and directing the greater portion of his concentration on the daylight that may come between the two combatants. By the time he could change his vision to a wider focus, the catcher would now be applying the swift tag. The umpire would have to use his judgment, snap a mental photo and come up with the call. It's only logical to assume that if a trace of obstruction did enter his mind, it's equally possible he had little or no time to digest the total picture of the obstruction phase of the play. He must actually *see* obstruction. It is difficult to deal with yourself after you have made a call that you can't justify 100 percent.

In any case, the chances of this play actually coming up are slim. However, after seeing this play, I thereafter continually *"looked on"* with an open mind when ruling on these particular situations. No doubt you will now be able to have the same insight and be prepared to recognize catcher's obstruction like an old pro.

Incidentally, the play I described ended with no argument and absolutely no one was aware of what transpired, except yours truly.

Ball Sticks in Screen
7.05H

It's safe to say we have all witnessed a batted ball that sticks in the protective screening surrounding spectators. Occasionally, a fan on the opposite side of the fence manages to claw at the prospective souvenir and finally maneuver the ball to pop through to *his side* of the fence. The surrounding fans applaud the effort and have a good laugh as the Johnny-on-the-spot ball boy is left looking on in vain, watching the ball disappear into the lucky grasp of the aggressive fan.

This is part of the game, make no mistake about it! Fans dream about the chance of capturing a baseball for a game souvenir. With the above situation in mind, I would occasionally call "Time" and give the youngster or adult a few more precious moments to pull the ball through and feel the joy of the accomplishment. From what I've seen, this fan who is trying like hell to get that ball is under spontaneous pressure. The ball boy, on the screen's other side, will amost always be there, waiting for a momentary lapse on the fan's part. At the same time, the umpire is supposed to be getting annoyed at the holdup. In addition to

Ball Sticks in Screen
Rule 7.05 (h)

7.05 Each runner including the batter-runner may, without liability to be put out, advance—

(h) One base, if a ball, pitched to the batter, or thrown by the pitcher from his position on the pitcher's plate to a base to catch a runner, goes into a stand or a bench, or over or through a field fence or backstop. The ball is dead.

that, how about the crowd's expectations. They are cheering encouragement for the youngster to pull off the caper; and nobody wants to be disappointed. This fun part of the game is all well and good . . . until the situation arises when the ball is alive!

Having been on both sides of the fence, let me give you a little insight as to what exactly can happen. Of course, the ball must be heading toward a fence opening approximately the same size as the sphere. The ball will most likely have its greatest portion sticking out on the field side. That means it would take only a simple tug from the catcher to pry the wedged ball loose from the screen, and by doing this the catcher would once again regain control of the situation on the field. However, spectators do not react objectively when a souvenir is at stake. Fans will express their selfishness by interfering with a fielder in order to *get that ball!* Players, managers and umpires are aware of this, and if the home team receives the short end of the stick, you can bet that particular fan who interfered will be more than sorry for his spontaneity. The fans in his section will, of course, embarrass him for his actions, and quite possibly the stadium police will be more than willing to escort him out of the park.

To eliminate this possibility, the rules clearly stipulate that once a ball sticks in a fence, the ball is dead and bases are awarded to the runners to justify the umpire's call of a dead ball. The call is the same as a ball entering the dugout or bounding into the stands. Even though the fielder will usually have the advantage of pulling the ball back out on his side, he might encounter spectator resistance. The rule is extremely logical, and the award of bases is true to how the situation would normally end up. In cases where the ball sticks from a *pitched ball* (see illustration) the award shall be *one* base from the time of the pitch. In cases where this happens and it is a first play by an infielder, the award is *two* bases from the time of the pitch. *In all other cases* the award is *two* bases from the time of the *throw!* Fans are continuously confused about how and why bases are awarded. You would be surprised to learn how many big leaguers are in the same boat!

Professional umpires are experts on the rules and on how to award bases. They very rarely rule incorrectly on the proper award.

Rebounding Foul Tip
Rule 6.05B

I am always very quick to correct anyone who misuses the terms *foul ball* and *foul tip*. I am not sure why I feel the constant need to clarify the differences, as most people don't care which is which. In ruling on the two, however, they are as different as you and I.

It is most important to remember that a foul ball is followed by the call of "Time"—automatically! Runners need not rush back to their respective bases in fear of being tagged out while off base. As a matter of fact, the ball should not be put back in play until all runners re-touch their original bases. Question: A hitter swings, barely tips the ball and the ball eludes the grasp of the catcher. Is it a foul ball or a foul tip? It is a foul ball! A foul tip can only result from a ball that is tipped and goes sharp and direct from the bat to the catcher's hands and is legally caught. Rebounds are acceptable to attain the foul tip ruling, but only after the ball has touched the catcher's free or glove hand first.

An embarrassing moment came one afternoon while I was umpiring the bases in the Carolina League in 1977. My partner, Mike Bender, was behind the plate. Since we were working a two-man system, I was in the middle of the infield with runners on first and third with two outs. The 2-2 pitch was swung at and tipped. The ball went directly off the bat, deflected off the catcher's glove, and rebounded off the catcher's protector where it was smothered by the quick-thinking receiver. The catcher raised his glove, with the ball located in the glove's pocket, and Mike peered over his shoulder to see if indeed the catcher had control. Mike determined that he had finally attained control, indicating foul tip by a hand signal, then proceeded to call "strike 3."

The teams started moving to change sides. However, in the meantime, here comes The Flying Bird Man, Zach Rebackoff, screaming "No, no, foul ball, Mike, foul ball!" I came running in toward home plate, frantically waving my arms indicating Mike had been screened. I was going to prove this umpiring crew works to get the call right.

When I was finally within earshot distance, Mike, obviously puzzled, asked "Zach, what the hell is the matter with you?"

"Nothing, Mike," I responded, "Just that the catcher smothered the ball against his chest. He never caught it clean. It went off his glove, then he smothered it. It's a foul ball." After listening to myself repeat the words, "It went off his glove," I then realized I was ready for Bellevue.

Not only was I wrong in my interpretational outburst, but equally wrong to overrule another umpire without first being asked for my opinion. Mike was a fairly levelheaded man and smiled at the whole scenario. He told both teams I had momentarily misunderstood the rule and the original call was official. (The General Manager phoned Bellevue and cancelled the emergency.)

In retrospect, I can honestly say that I was never in doubt of the rule, only briefly confused by seeing the rebound from the infield. Without giving the play enough consideration, I foolishly blurted out my erroneous reaction. A foul tip can actually rebound any number of times, as long as it rebounds off the catcher. The ball must first go sharp and direct off either of the catcher's hands and never once touch the batter, umpire, or any foreign object including the ground. It is highly unlikely that the ball will rebound off the catcher to one of his teammates unless one of the infielders is playing way in for a bunt. The ball may even rebound off the

Rebounding Foul Tip

Rule 6.05 (b)

6.05 A batter is out when—

(b) A third strike is legally caught by the catcher;

"Legally caught" means in the catcher's glove before the ball touches the ground. It is not legal if the ball lodges in his clothing or paraphernalia; or if it touches the umpire and is caught by the catcher on the rebound.

If a foul-tip first strikes the catcher's glove and then goes on through and is caught by both hands against his body or protector, before the ball touches the ground, it is a strike, and if third strike, batter is out. If smothered against his body or protector, it is a catch provided the ball struck the catcher's glove or hand first.

shinguards (first hitting the glove or hand, of course) and still be considered a foul tip.

Broadcasters, in general, are guilty of using the wrong vocabulary to describe this situation. Now that all of you have read this section, you will not be falsely informed again. You now know heads from tails, which is more than I can say for the broadcasters who want you to believe they know it all.

Second Play by an Infielder
Rule 7.05G

The situation I am about to describe was among the most controversial of my entire career and has still not been satisfactorily resolved . . . in my opinion. Unfortunately our president, Harold Cooper, would not budge from his interpretation of Rule 7.05G. This situation is complicated and needs to be clarified at length.

This rule was always on my mind, and still is, more than ever. The problem is, this wordy rule fails to define what the word "play" means. When you think about the word *play,* you logically assume that it means the completion of one . . . play! What else can you say? That's exactly what I assume the Rules Committee had in mind. Who would think that the actual act or incomplete act of a play would generate a great amount of confusion when bases were to be awarded much less in determining if it is a first play or a second play? A play is a play, right? That's what I thought. Not true.

In 1982, Jack Lietz, an International League umpire in his ninth pro season, was working, as I was, in the I.L. However, we were not on the same crew when this rarity took place. Jack was involved in a particular incident that deserves considerable explanation in this chapter.

With a runner on first and moving on the pitch, the batter grounded to the shortstop who moved to his left, filling the hole and cutting off the potential base hit. After snaring the hard-bounding ball, he looked to force the runner at second by taking it himself. After examining his chances of beating the lead runner, he reconsidered his course of action and contemplated a quick toss to the alert and covering second baseman. Again, after careful consideration and deciding he'd be late with that "play," too, he fired to first to try and salvage the only remaining out possible. His throw was wild and three rows up in the crowd!

Now, did he make a play on the lead runner or not? Was the wild throw the first play by our infielder or the second? Let's backtrack a minute. Lietz claims the shortstop committed himself twice in trying to force the lead man. After he fielded the ball, Jack continued, he took a couple of steps towards second! In other words, he entertained the thought of proceeding to race the runner to the bag. Then he very definitely indicated, by preparing to flip to the second baseman, that he wanted to force the runner. He again chose not to, as he anticipated the toss would be late, then finally threw on to first. In addition, Jack claimed that the runner had already reached second by the time the relay to first was released. So, of course, Jack awarded the lead runner home, and the batter-runner second. I agree with his award totally—if the shortstop's first set of actions are considered a play.

The defense protested the decision (the offense scored the tying run on the play) and when it passed the league president's desk, he shockingly upheld the *appeal*. I say shockingly, because of his interpretation of the rule in question. A few days later, Cooper personally asked my opinion of the play and for my interpretation. I told him that if in Jack's judgment he considered the act of the shortstop to be a play, then he ruled correctly and courageously.

Cooper kept referring back to one small phrase from this section of the rules. The paragraph starting with "The position of the batter-runner at the time the throw left the thrower's hand is the key in deciding the award of bases." As you continue to read the

© COPYRIGHT 1985 ZACK ABRAHROFF

Second Play by an Infielder
Rule 7.05 (g)

7.05 Each runner including the batter-runner may, without liability to be put out, advance—

(g) Two bases when, with no spectators on the playing field, a thrown ball goes into the stands, or into a bench (whether or not the ball rebounds into the field), or over or under or through a field fence, or on a slanting part of the screen above the backstop, or remains in the meshes of a wire screen protecting spectators. The ball is dead. When such wild throw is the first play by an infielder, the umpire, in awarding such bases, shall be governed by the position of the runners at the time the ball was pitched; in all other cases the umpire shall be governed by the position of the runners at the time the wild throw was made;

APPROVED RULING: If all runners, including the batter-runner, have advanced at least one base when an infielder makes a wild throw on the first play after the pitch, the award shall be governed by the position of the runners when the wild throw was made.

In certain circumstances it is impossible to award a runner two bases. Example: Runner on first. Batter hits fly to short right. Runner holds up between first and second and batter comes around first and pulls up behind him. Ball falls safely. Outfielder, in throwing to first, throws ball into stand.

APPROVED RULING: Since no runner, when the ball is dead, may advance beyond the base to which he is entitled, the runner originally on first base goes to third base and the batter is held at second base.

The term "when the wild throw was made" means when the throw actually left the player's hand and not when the thrown ball hit the ground, passes a receiving fielder or goes out of play into the stands.

The position of the batter-runner at the time the wild throw left the thrower's hand is the key in deciding the award of bases. If the batter-runner has not reached first base, the award is two bases at the time the pitch was made for all runners. The decision as to whether the batter-runner has reached first base before the throw is a judgment call.

If an unusual play arises where a first throw by an infielder goes into stands or dugout but the batter did not become a runner (such as catcher throwing ball into stands in attempt to get runner from third trying to score on passed ball or wild pitch) award of two bases shall be from the position of the runners at the time of the throw. (For the purpose of Rule 7.05 (g) a catcher is considered an infielder.)

PLAY: Runner on first base, batter hits a ball to the shortstop, who throws to second base too late to get runner at second, and second baseman throws toward first base after batter has crossed first base. Ruling—Runner at second scores. (On this play, only if batter-runner is past first base when throw is made is he awarded third base.)

complete paragraph, you will at first agree that Cooper has a point! But wait, see my logic for a moment. I have been a student of the rules for almost 10 years now, dissecting them constantly. In my opinion, this small phrase deals with *first throws by an infielder!* As you can see in the first paragraph, the rule specifically informs you about wild throws on the first play by an infielder and defines the awarding of bases for all runners from the time of the pitch. The rule then declares that *"In all other cases the award of bases shall be dictated by the position of the runners at the time the wild throw was made."* Obviously, a new and a more careful look at the wording is necessary.

Getting back to Cooper, he would not fully consider the overwhelming evidence against his ruling to uphold the appeal. Cooper did, in fact, say that he was not questioning Jack's judgment on whether a play was or was not executed—this is yet another story. So why did he rule in favor of the protesting team? Because, of that small *"key"* phrase.

This play is not your everyday routine baseball situation. A protest on this rarity is not surprising. After all, managers and players are not students of the rules, and are expected to question unusual plays or rulings. What *was* surprising, however, was the fact that Cooper upheld the protest and ordered the game to be resumed at a later date with runners on second and third. I have to question his reasoning as he sought out and received other professional opinions (a good many favoring Jack's award) before coming to his final decision. After listening to opposing views and going along with the umpire's declaration that a first play had transpired, Cooper still ruled against the umpires.

About two weeks passed, and yours truly was working second base when yet another "second play" type of situation arose. My situation was a clear-cut play, however, but nonetheless created a decision on awarding bases. Of course, I ruled as I would have before or after the "Lietz deal." I gave the lead runner home (see the illustration; the runner clearly was on the bag before the release) and the batter-runner second. No argument or protest was made, but Cooper was listening to the game from Columbus on radio. He was on the horn at 9 a.m. the next morning complaining that we had not followed his previous directive for this situation. Our crew had Umpire Development Supervisor Barney Deary call Cooper with his opinion—which agreed with ours. Nothing doing! Cooper would only change his decision when and if the Rules Committee officially ruled differently.

This prompted Cooper to mail out a strong directive to the league's staff of umpires, stating that all umpires would rule on this play as he wanted until the Rules Committee could clear up this whole controversy. I couldn't believe it! The boss actually wanted his umpires to rule contrary to their interpretation of the official playing rules. This umpire could not understand why Cooper had to validate his ruling with what in my opinion was a total misconception. His theory was that in awarding bases, the umpires should give runners two bases from their position at the time of the pitch. Cooper indicated that the Rules Committee would review the play, then get back to the league and entire National Association with its findings.

How long would that take? The play could happen in any given game, right? Was the whole umpiring staff ready to rule on what they knew was wrong? I wasn't! At the very least I didn't want to. How could this be happening? How could the entire National Association, which had been alerted to this inept paraphrasing, stand by and wait until the Committee was prepared to deal with this peculiarity?—especially the part that is unclear about what constitutes a play. I felt, and still do, that a official ruling from the Rules Committee was in order . . . as soon as possible!

Later that season I was in transit through New York's LaGuardia airport, when I happened to run into the National League's very large and very sharp John McSherry. McSherry is a bona fide major league umpire. We talked for awhile about the usual, then I remembered to ask him about the *play*. I asked John now he would define the word "play" in this particular case. His answer was miraculous. He said that he would consider an act "a play" when the umpire in turn needs to *make a call*. In other words, in referring to Lietz's play, since the shortstop never did actually force a call from the umpire it was not a play! McSherry definitely has the right perspective, and one that I am now prepared to proclaim as my own.

I argued this point with Mr. Cooper through written communication, as well as in person. Maybe Cooper took it personally, I'm not sure. He said he respected my stand, yet he was the league president. Need I say more? I hope you didn't hold it against me, Coop.

At the time of this writing I have not been informed of any new changes on this particular situation. The 1983 official playing rules have not been revised in regard to what is actually a "play." Baseball is indeed a funny game.

Infield Fly
Rule 2.00

It was at umpire school that I really learned the definition of the *Infield Fly Rule.* I was coached on the prerequisites that precede the apparently cut and dried rule—"Less than two outs, runners on first and second or bases loaded, and a pop-up (bunts, even though they might be popped up, are not considered within the guidelines of an infield fly) that can be handled by an infielder with ordinary effort." It all seemed quite simple until I was actually confronted with game and weather conditions.

I disciplined myself not to vocally express my brilliance and recognize an infield fly too quickly. On a windy day (night), every pop fly is an adventure. Many times, as the ball goes off the bat skyward, players from the defensive team would reassure each other not to panic, as the infield fly rule was in effect—not fully realizing that the *umpire* is the *only* one who can actually declare "Infield Fly."

Now, remember this: Putting the infield fly rule into effect, immediately puts an out on the scoreboard. Our hasty arbiter is going to look foolish if the wind keeps swooping and swirling and forces the infielder to ride the wind to keep a beat on the continuously slicing ball—only to run out of hope and have the ball fall untouched or dropped. At this time I will take the

© COPYRIGHT 1983 ZACH REBACKOFF

142

Infield Fly
Rule 2.00

2.00 An INFIELD FLY is a fair fly ball (not includilng a line drive nor an attempted bunt) which can be caught by an infielder with ordinary effort, when first and second, or first, second and third bases are occupied, before two are out. The pitcher, catcher and any outfielder who stations himself in the infield on the play shall be considered infielders for the purpose of this rule.

When it seems apparent that a batted ball will be an Infield Fly, the umpire shall immediately declare "Infield Fly" for the benefit of the runners. If the ball is near the baselines, the umpire shall declare "Infield Fly, if Fair."

The ball is alive and runners may advance at the risk of the ball being caught, or retouch and advance after the ball is touched, the same as on any fly ball. If the hit becomes a foul ball, it is treated the same as any foul.

If a declared Infield Fly is allowed to fall untouched to the ground, and bounces foul before passing first or third base, it is a foul ball. If a declared Infield Fly falls untouched to the ground outside the baseline, and bounces fair before passing first or third base, it is an Infield Fly.

On the infield fly rule the umpire is to rule whether the ball could ordinarily have been handled by an infielder—not by some arbitrary limitation such as the grass, or the base lines. The umpire must rule also that a ball is an infield fly, even if handled by an outfielder, if, in the umpire's judgment, the ball could have been as easily handled by an infielder. The infield fly is in no sense to be considered an appeal play. The umpire's judgment must govern, and the decision should be made immediately.

When an infield fly rule is called, runners may advance at their own risk. If on an infield fly rule, the infielder intentionally drops a fair ball, the ball remains in play despite the provisions of Rule 6.05 (L). The infield fly rule takes precedence.

opportunity to point out a personal conflict I find in the writing of the rules. On page 18 of the 1983 Official Baseball Rules, in the second paragraph dealing with the infield fly rule, it starts off by saying, "When it sems apparent that a batted ball will be an infield fly, the umpire shall immediately declare Infield Fly for the benefit of the runners." That is fine and I agree 100 percent. However, on page 19, while continuing to elaborate on that particular play (the infield fly) the rule book says, "The umpire's judgment must govern, and the decision should be made immediately."

Now, being a student of the rules and having had to enforce this rule countless times, I know I would never call an infield fly *immediately,* even when it first seems apparent. There are too many things that can change during the pop-up, and I have too much experience to jump to conclusions. In any case, for the average baseball fan who would like to learn the proper ruling and mechanics, this small contradiction would be confusing. How does one determine if ordinary effort is needed or not, until one has the opportunity to make a legitimate judgment based on viewing the ball's flight, the fielder's jump, and the use of general peripheral vision on the play?

Our extra-cool umpire will look like "Father Insight" by sliding along with the swirling wind (and ball) and by keeping his judgmental opinion to himself *until* the ball is on its way down, several feet from the fielder's mitt. If the ump sees that *more* than ordinary effort is needed to make the catch, there is no need to make the call. If and when the fielder draws a beat on the ball and ordinary effort is apparent, the umpire simply declares: "Infield fly, batter is out!" If the ball is arcing down near either of the foul lines, the words "If Fair" are added to cover an untouched ball landing and staying on foul territory.

Question: If an infielder is comfortably backpedaling under an infield fly, and the umpire has declared it an *infield fly,* what would happen if an onrushing outfielder calls him off and decides to make the catch himself? To add to this dilemma, suppose he collides with his teammate or miscalculates the ball's flight and the ball falls to the ground—all this occurring *after* the umpire called it an infield fly? Confusion, right? Wrong. It's still ruled an infield fly! The batter is out, and runners may run at their own risk.

Question: When the infield fly rule is in effect, are the runners in jeopardy to be put out (if they do indeed run) by a *force* or *tag* play? Cute, eh? It's a tag situation. Remember, I told you they can run only if they want. If the force was on, they would *have to run*.

In summation, an apparently easy call can bring to mind constant judgmental changes during a mere pop fly. The official must continually evaluate the balls' flight plus the changing plight of the infielder to determine the simplicity of ordinary effort. The point to remember here is to wait—wait until the ball is descending or even inches from the glove, if necessary. Don't call it until you are positive it is an infield fly.

Catch in Dugout
Rule 7.04C

It is difficult to explain why this rule is not followed consistently throughout professional baseball. I learned that this particular ground rule would be set forth at the home team's discretion, making it necessary to stipulate the exact rule before each series of games that took place.

In accordance with the rules, dead ball territory may differ from one ballpark to another which, of course, presents the problem of setting down ground rules for each particular stadium. That is understandable as no two fields are exactly alike. However, dugouts are present at every professional playing field. Why do some stadiums permit catches in the dugout and others not?

One explanation is that dugouts vary in their length, depth and level of danger. Each major league franchise owns a minor league farm system. The teams compete in a league with the principal purpose being the development of their future major league stars. It would be illogical for the players to endanger their futures by risking injury through ill-considered heroics. A player can be evaluated in every relevant category without inflicting undue risks in the process.

Fully developed major leaguers are paid large sums of money to go all-out to catch everything in sight. Obviously, to catch a ball that is nearing the dugout steps takes a good deal of concentration and dedication to the cause. I once saw Minnesota's catcher, Earl Battey inflict such pain on himself it was incredible. The man completely disregarded his own safety by charging full steam for a foul pop-up near the dugout. His momentum carried him directly into the dugouts horizontal protective bars which stopped him dead—by the neck! This play took place in the 1965 World Series and Battey was carried off on a stretcher.

That play is an indication of what is in store for any player who plays without regard to injury. All major league stadiums play under the rule stated in this section, 7.04C. A player may be held up physically be either team while attempting to enter the dugout to make the play. As long as the catch is made and he does not *fall down inside,* the ball remains alive and in play.

Reviewing this situation during my active career, I cannot remember any major injury occurring on my field due to a player utilizing the dugout to snare a loose pop-up.

However, I have seen too many *near-casualties* because of the ever-present danger of accidentally tripping or falling down the steps. In my opinion it is foolish to keep the dugout in play to make catches. Why risk cracking someone's head open for a pop-up? Even the most consistent hitters make an out 70 percent of the time. The rule is slightly inconsistent because in all other situations that evolve around a ball entering the dugout, the ball immediately becomes dead. And that's a fact! If a thrown ball could be retrieved inside the dugout by going in and locating it, I would consider *that* more logical. The player could plan his hasty approach and the injury risk would be lowered considerably. This still would not be a good idea because you can bet your last dollar if the ball was to be located in the offense's dugout, the player would encounter numerous problems crawling through immobilized players. This is one of the reasons that live balls become dead once they enter the dugout.

© COPYLIGHT 1983 ZACH REBACKOFF

Catch in Dugout
Rule 7.04 (c)

7.04 Each runner, other than the batter, may without liability to be put out, advance one base when—

(c) A fielder, after catching a fly ball, falls into a bench or stand, or falls across ropes into a crowd when spectators are on the field;

A fielder or catcher may reach or step into, or go into the dugout with one or both feet to make a catch, and if he holds the ball, the catch shall be allowed. Ball is in play.

If the fielder or catcher, after having made a legal catch, should fall into a stand or among spectators or into the dugout after making a legal catch, or fall while in the dugout after making a legal catch, the ball is dead and runners advance one base without liability to put out.

The dugouts, in my opinion, are out of play, and should be kept that way to ensure safety for all players at all levels of baseball. There is room for improvement regarding this rule and I sincerely hope that a serious injury is not the catalyst for a change.

Batted Ball Rebounds off Rubber
Rule 2.00 Foul Ball
(3rd Paragraph)

I would not consider this play in the category headed "most unusual plays." Granted, it is unusual, but I have witnessed crazier. This play does, however, have its place in the heart of trivia experts. Just looking at the play (see illustration) your first impression is that *it is a fair ball!*

In constructing an *imaginary boundary line* for determining when a ball is to be adjudged *fair,* and meet no other requirements, the bases themselves serve this purpose. To clarify what I just told you, picture a pop-up that falls in behind the mound. The ball has such an extraordinary spin on it that it actually spins itself back toward the first base foul line and finally settles in foul territory. Fair or foul? It's foul! If the pop-up had reached the imaginary lines of the basepaths, (a direct line from one base to another) and touched down in fair territory, the ball could spin itself clear to China. It would still be ruled fair.

The illustration shown here in Rule 2.00, third paragraph, has got to be confusing to the game's managers and players. Confus-

Batted Ball Rebounds off Rubber
Rule 2.00 Foul Ball (3rd Paragraph)

2.00 Foul Ball (3rd Paragraph)

A batted ball not touched by a fielder, which hits the pitcher's rubber and rebounds into foul territory, between home and first, or between home and third base is a foul ball.

ing because this play would be ruled simply a *foul ball!* The pitcher's rubber, raised higher than the natural ground and height of the mound, presents an illusion that induces one to believe the ball is immediately fair on contact. Maybe it's the pinpoint accuracy of the hit that causes everyone to believe that the hitter should not be punished for placing such a perfect line drive. It was, after all, right up the middle! Another reason for skepticism may be because of the sudden change of direction the ball takes on. We should not forget that the rubber is part of the field and should be treated as such. Even at this moment of writing, I visualize the play over and over and still find it mind-boggling that it is a foul ball. But believe me, it is!

In making the call of *foul,* it is imperative that the deciding umpire be sure the ball did not touch the pitcher or his glove—before or after the ball contacted the rubber. If it had, it would definitely be a fair ball. After assuring himself of that factor, next he must be positive of the position of the ball when it enters the first baseman's grasp. Additionally, he must be certain that the catch does not occur beyond the bag, as that would constitute a fair and live ball. If the ricocheted ball crosses any portion of the bag, it would be ruled fair. This all transpires in a matter of about 1½ seconds. Umpiring, as you see, is not an easy gig. Granted, there are a number of plays that call themselves, but the real weird plays take a lot of composure and experience to call correctly. It is quite normal for a ballgame to be moving along routinely, and then all of a sudden—bang! The play is on you! This is where the umpires earn their money. They have got to jump on the call quickly, accurately and aggressively, to alleviate any doubt that is presented by the rare ricochet.

Obstruction
Rule 7.06

The act of obstruction is one situation that cannot be cast as a cut and dried rule, or for that matter be interpreted as such. Although the rule book specifies what obstruction *is* and how it should be dealt with, it is still one of the most confusing interpretations to have to make. You can ask 10 umpires the ruling on the very same obstruction play, and receive 8 to 10 different answers. Obstruction is a highly judgmental observation, which needs to be sorted out in one's mind within a second. That is not much time to be conclusive on a play where the penalty does not always end up logically.

Let me first explain what I mean by "logically." Example: A batter drives a long single to left-center. He rounds first, and is contemplating trying to turn the basehit into a double. After making a very big turn around first, he realizes the outfielder covered his ground expertly and has made a fine play in cutting off the potential two-bagger. The outfielder then sets himself, and fires a strong peg to second. The runner, now positive he cannot

Obstruction
Rule 7.06

7.06 When obstruction occurs, the umpire shall call or signal "Obstruction."

(a) If a play is being made on the obstructed runner, or if the batter-runner is obstructed before he touches first base, the ball is dead and all runners shall advance, without liability to be put out, to the bases they would have reached, in the umpire's judgment, if there had been no obstruction. The obstructed runner shall be awarded at least one base beyond the base he had last legally touched before the obstruction. Any preceding runners, forced to advance by the award of bases as the penalty for obstruction, shall advance without liability to be put out.

make second safely, puts on the brakes, and as quickly as he can, retraces his steps in hopes of returning to the safety of first.

The second baseman now sees he has a play on the speedster and sets to relay to first. In returning to first base, the runner runs directly into the pitcher, who is now in the *basepaths* because it's his job to back up the incoming throw from the outfield. The first baseman is awaiting the relay to apply a quick tag. After the collision, caused by the pitcher's presence, the runner regains his balance and continues to dig for first. However, his effort is in vain as the awaiting first baseman easily applies the tag for the putout.

Our first base umpire is fully aware of the extra burden inflicted on the daring baserunner. He was clearly trying to make it back to first and settle for his single, yet the rules clearly stipulate that the runner is to be awarded at least one base beyond the last base he had legally touched. This runner is awarded second! This does not make sense to me. The runner is lucky if he made it back to first. For argument's sake, say no obstruction had occurred and he would (given the benefit of the doubt) have gotten back to first safely. Why award him second? His goal was to re-attain first, and he was obstructed from reaching his goal. Most umpires agree that this rule is not consistent with other baserunning awards. I have tried to figure out the reasoning behind this rule and have come up with this. In my opinion, the rule was written to cover the runners obstructed while advancing, not returning to, bases. However, in reading the rule, the umpire has no choice but to award the additional base. Readers, be prepared for another George Brett Pine-Tar type controversy. It's gonna happen, and the league and its umpires will again be caught in a contradictory rule situation. Again the spirit of the rule will be questioned.

Continuing one step further, there is a possibility that could develop where the umpire *can declare obstruction,* yet need not make an award of bases to the obstructed runner. Example: The hitter lines a clean single to right field. While rounding first base, he is obstructed by the first baseman. However, in the umpire's judgment the runner had no intention of going for second. He only made a big turn to draw a throw to second. A play was not being made *directly* on the runner. The umpire should announce obstruction only to cover himself. In doing so, he eliminates the argument that he missed or failed to declare obstruction. If questioned, he can justify that not only did he see the contact, but made the players aware of that as well. In this particular situation, however, the contact *did not* interfere with the intentions of the runner, therefore, no penalty was enforced.

My experiences with obstructed runners have usually occurred when they are trying to advance to the next base. It is good common sense to realize that if obstruction does occur, all umpires should be aware of the pending circumstances. If a runner is obstructed while going from second to third and a play is made on him at third, an ensuing argument is assured if the umpire declares the runner *out,* then, changes his call to adapt to the award, because of the preceding obstruction. Why call him out in the first place? He is not out and never was! The call is not *out,* then *safe* because he was obstructed. The umpire simply calls "Time," and declares the runner safe because he was obstructed.

Obstruction situations are difficult for an inexperienced arbiter to recognize. Players move quickly and expertly across the diamond. Runners and fielders are both equally quilty of trying to create adversity by use of trickery. The umpires must see through this and be confident in their own judgment and observe the touchy situation with objectivity and fair play. Both teams will claim the other is at fault. If the umpire finds himself totally unaware of an obstruction, he must be prepared to consult with his crew to correct any problem that was overlooked by his momentary lack of concentration. Very often, a wider view of the play can be helpful in putting the play in its proper prospective.

In summation, I feel obliged to make my readers aware of the experience necessary to rule correctly on plays such as this with consistency. As an umpire, it is not necessary to immediately award bases. A couple of seconds to re-evaluate the last position of the runners is helpful and highly recommended. Get your story straight in your mind. It is definite that you will need to explain your entire position to the manager. The manager will go as far as telling the umpire that not only does he disagee his player was guilty of obstruction, but he believes offensive interference is the right call. The move is to be strong and confident . . . and I wish you luck!

Fielder Creates Unnatural Path for Ball to Roll Foul
Rule 9.01C

During the time I was toiling in the minor leagues, I was denied two things. One, of course, was being given an opportunity to umpire in the majors. The other was to rule on 9.01C! It just never came up. That would be a great experience as the ruling would undoubtedly get tossed around by the Rules Committee and finally positioned properly within the rule book. But, that's the way things go.

Nevertheless, I remember viewing a series of baseball highlights on TV one afternoon. This clip showed a major league third baseman actually blowing so hard on a dribbler down the line, that he was able to divert the 5 ¼ -ounce ball into foul territory— and the umpire called it foul! I believe the league sent out a special directive to all its umpires after this oddity, declaring that if a fielder were to try this tactic in the future, the ball should be ruled fair. After all, the play is rather devious, don't you agree?

The rules prohibit the offense from intentional or unintentional interference, so why not penalize this perpetrator for devising his own method of interference?

Remaining within the play in question here, the third baseman

Fielder Creates Unnatural Path for Ball to Roll Foul
Rule 9.01 (c)

9.01 (c) Each umpire has authority to rule on any point not specifically covered in these rules.

(or any fielder for that matter) can induce a rolling ball to go foul by regressing to his childhood days in the sandbox. By forming a groove in the basepath's dirt he will cause the ball to roll easily into and follow the curved path and ultimately find its way to foul territory. Again, this play will not be specifically mentioned in the rule book. However, it is not condoned by professional baseball. The umpire should rule in favor of the offense again and call the ball *fair*. By quoting rule 9.01C, the umpire can successfully maintain the integrity of the game and not allow the game to turn into a farce.

Up until 1977, the official rule book contained a case book section. This section was filled with additional interpretations or elaborations on particular rules. Additional rule revisions were also placed in this section as the years went by. In 1977, to provide its readers with quicker access to any of the written language in the book, the "Case Book" section was added directly into the rules in the relevant positions. This gives the reader easier application of a particular rule. I find it odd that both of the plays I outlined in this section are *still* not included. The Rules Committee is quite surprising and quite beyond me. Not one of the committee's 10 members is an umpire! All are bona fide baseball executives. However, none have had the on-the-field pressure of ruling on plays.

A major league umpire could certainly bring a deeper insight to the committee room. I feel it is an injustice to the game as well as an insult to major league umpires to not include the opinions of the men who enforce the rules and maintain the integrity of the game. There are an additional two members on the committee who are in an "advisory position." Still, no major league or ex-major league umpire! I do not see the logic of closing the door to the men who are faced with enforcing the rules. Who would know the rules better than a prominent rules man from the Major Leagues Umpires Association? I think I know the answer: NO ONE!

In summation, it is safe to say that rule 9.01C is rarely used to solve the daily problems facing baseball umpires. I'll tell you one thing, though: I'm sure glad it's there. You never know!

Ground-Rule Double; (Ball Through Fence)
Rule 7.05F

Everyone that knows the basic baseball rules can tell you what a "ground-rule double" is. Sure, it's a fairly batted ball that bounces over the outfield fence. Everyone would be right.

But let's place our umpiring crew in this spot. There is a runner on first, two-out, and he is stealing on the pitch. He is only 30 to 35 feet from second when the batter belts a long drive, 396 feet from home plate. Listen man, with two outs and the runners going, even Boss Steinbrenner would reach home easily. So, why not rule logically on this play. The offense was on their toes by stealing on the pitch and the batter did his job so, in a nutshell, the offense deserves the run! They worked superbly to make it. An apparently undeniable injustice! I see their point.

But wait a second. Are we (the umpires) going to be placed in this critical position every time the ball bounces, goes through, or is deflected into the stands? Umpires would have to start clocking runners to determine who was gifted to the point of reaching an extra base. I think not! Our job is to follow the game, not lead. The Rules Committee can be applauded on this general ruling, by narrowing the options to one. Let the next guy drive them in!

Ground-Rule Double;
(Ball Through Fence)
Rule 7.05 (f)

7.05 Each runner including the batter-runner may, without liability to be put out, advance—

(f) Two bases, if a fair ball bounces or is deflected into the stands outside the first or third base foul lines; or if it goes through or under a field fence, or through or under a scoreboard, or through or under shrubbery or vines on the fence; or if it sticks in such fence, scoreboard, shrubbery or vines.

162

The Cap Catch
Rule 7.05B

At certain times I find myself wondering why specific rules were written into the rule book in the first place. This one has got to be on almost everyone's list. Why would a player even attempt to pull off this prank? All the odds are against him.

Actually, there is a small area of logic for using this manuever. Consider: a player has realized that in order to prevent a hit the *only* way to keep the ball from going through or past him would be to attain the extra few inches that an extended cap could give him. Even the quickest thinking players would have trouble coming up with this solution under pressure. In my opinion, this is the most likely reason for the rules entry.

One other reason for one to try this play would be for the entertainment of the crowd. It would be a "pretty play" for an outfielder to casually lift off his cap, camp under a 300-foot drive and snare it out of thin air. It would be safe to assume that if one could pull in a fly ball with his cap, he would certainly be able to put it away using his glove. So why then penalize the team for

The Cap Catch
Rule 7.05 (b)

7.05 Each runner including the batter-runner may, without liability to be put out, advance—

(b) Three bases, if a fielder deliberately touches a fair ball with his cap, mask or any part of his uniform detached from its proper place on his person. The ball is in play and the batter may advance to home base at his peril.

this? Because, you have to draw the line on what constitutes a last-ditch attempt, in comparison to a flair for the dramatics. The rule focuses on consistency, and will tolerate neither circumstance.

When I first read about this rule, I was attending umpire school. I was dying to pull off this caper in our practice sessions. All students participated in simulated baseball situations while other students rotated as umpires. I realized that if I decided to utilize this trick play, I could possibly create a bit of confusion for the unsuspecting student-umpire. I would hate to make him rule incorrectly because of my flair for the dramatics. However, how could these same students not be ready to rule on such an oddity when they were studying the rules daily? I would probably make him look good as he could jump right on it and impress our group instructor and A.L. umpire, Nick Bremigan. That clinched it! I was ready.

The next day my opportunity was before me, as I was playing center field on a bright sunny morning in St. Petersburg, Fla. Bremigan was again our instructor. (Incidentally, Nick Bremigan is the best rules man I've ever spoken with. I respect his opinion immensely in regard to the Official Playing Rules). I had decided that the next routine fly ball hit to me would be the time for the "catch." Sure enough, a nice lofty fly ball was headed right to me. My heart skipped as I took off my cap to hip level, and gingerly cushioned the impact of riding the force with a backward sweeping motion. That sucker landed smack in the center of my blue cap! The "Say Hey Kid" couldn't have topped that one!!

Nick Bremigan wanted to strangle me. He was perturbed, to say the least. (He tried to conceal his own amusement but had a difficult time). "Rebackoff," he shouted, "start running." (Whenever students did something moronic or committed an error in ethics, the usual penalty was to take a lap or two around the entire field. Ingenious method of teaching!) I assumed Bremigan pegged me in the "moronic" category. He displayed a moment of irritation and informed me that I was to continue to jog until lunch. Hell, that was half an hour away! I never dreamed I would be punished so severely.

To this day, I still remember the self-satisfaction and admiration I gave myself for the great individual accomplishment. If you think it's easy, try it sometime. You'll notice that a substantial amount of concentration and calculation is needed, not to mention the pressure from fear of dropping the ball. That is embarrassment with a capital E. This trick is nice for a gag, but certainly is not worth the three bases you give up if you really go for it. My advice? Go for it, it's great! By the way, I must apologize to the student umpire I inadvertantly chose. My immaturity and selfishness blinded my common sense. My advice *now* to umpire school students? Still go for it!

Fielder falls into stands after making catch
Rule 7.04C

Spectacular catches are one of the most appreciated feats in baseball. I remember times when even I have been amazed at the effort involved in order to make a great catch. Being on the field night after night, one gets accustomed to seeing *good* plays, but a great play is something that takes guts and coordination.

When fielders catch a ball and then fall into the stands, it usually happens in foul territory. The player realizes he may be in for a scrap with the spectators, but has decided to give up his body and soul for the purpose of bringing back with him, the out! Since I make a habit of ruling on unusual plays, I can only sympathize with the defense in the play illustrated in this section.

Say there's one out, a runner on third and a high pop-up is hit down the left field line (just past third base) and nearing the stands. Not really deep enough for the runner to tag on, it's a difficult play for the third baseman, shortstop or left fielder who's coming way in.

Fielder falls into stands after making catch
Rule 7.04 (c)

7.04 Each runner, other than the batter, may without liability to be put out, advance one base when—

(c) A fielder, after catching a fly ball, falls into a bench or stand, or falls across ropes into a crowd when spectators are on the field;

A fielder or catcher may reach or step into, or go into the dugout with one or both feet to make a catch, and if he holds the ball, the catch shall be allowed. Ball is in play.

If the fielder or catcher, after having made a legal catch, should fall into a stand or among spectators or into the dugout after making a legal catch, or fall while in the dugout after making a legal catch, the ball is dead and runners advance one base without liability to put out.

Players are conditioned from the time they put on their first baseball cap to *catch that ball*—almost at all costs. It is good intent and will benefit his team the majority of the time. As you can see by the illustration, this man made a fantastic catch. He has even kept his cool by realizing the runner would take advantage of his mishap and tag up. Being an all-round athlete, he regains his balance and fires a perfect strike to the plate, for an apparent inning-ending double play.

The third baseman obviously turned in an extraordinary play, and deserves all the credit in the world for his talent, intelligence and perseverance. The rules, however, in this particular case, have worked against him and his team. I still agree with the present rule. It must be assumed that this rule still gives the defense an advantage. If this were a crowd of hungry, involved fans, they could easily continue to apprehend the overturned player, therefore turning the basepaths into an everlasting turnstile to register runs. By pinning him down, or trying to steal the ball the fans could easily win the game on a mere foul pop. In more cases than not, this rule prevents fan participation, and gives each team an equal amount of protection as far as baserunners are concerned.

OFFENSIVE PLAY

Pitch Hits Batter in Strike Zone
Rule 6.08B

Once upon a time there was a universally known baseball player, who was heralded for his tremendous all-around talent. He was in fact so great, that a vast majority of the baseball world considered him the greatest player of all time. He smacked hundreds of home runs, swiped countless bases with his great speed and skill, made catches that only the gods could have made, and generated team enthusiasm like no other.

This great player had one more additional characteristic. He would take his normal batting stance unusually close to home plate. He was, therefore, hit with more than a normal share of baseballs. You know who it is? His name is Willie Mays, the ''Say Hey Kid.''

Now Willie did not need charity by relying on reaching base by taking one on the arm. He was, in his time, one of the game's superstars and could drive the ball all over the field with authority! Yet Mays did crouch close to the plate and took his lumps more than occasionally. Nothing, not even an apparent knockdown pitch, could move Willie off the plate.

© COPYRIGHT 1985 IMR RESEARCH

Pitch Hits Batter in Strike Zone
Rule 6.08 (b)

6.08 The batter becomes a runner and is entitled to first base without liability to be put out (provided he advances to and touches first base) when—

(b) He is touched by a pitched ball which he is not attempting to hit unless (1) The ball is in the strike zone when it touches the batter, or (2) The batter makes no attempt to avoid being touched by the ball;

If the ball is in the strike zone when it touches the batter, it shall be called a strike, whether or not the batter tries to avoid the ball. If the ball is outside the strike zone when it touches the batter, it shall be called a ball if he makes no attempt to avoid being touched.

APPROVED RULING: When the batter is touched by a pitched ball which does not entitle him to first base, the ball is dead and no runner may advance.

Willie Mays was not the first or last person to crowd the plate. Minnie Minoso and Frank Robinson were famous for getting hit by pitches. It is the hitter's priority to claim any part of the batter's box he feels most comfortable in. The consequences are frightening when you realize the ball can take you down at 90–100 mph. Increasing your danger by being on top of the plate, is not my idea of "being comfortable."

From the home plate umpire's point of view, it is much more difficult to see the ball zooming in, and judge the pitch for a strike or ball. The ump must adjust from his normal position to be able to see *clearly*. By having the batter crouch *that* close to the plate, it takes away a small area used to judge the inside corner.

When this situation does come into play, the umpire must be on his toes for the pitch that tails inside close to the hands. This brings us to an additional problem. Did the ball hit the hands or the bat? The bottom knob of the bat is usually close to or even with the hitter's bottom finger. When the pitch comes inside, the ball may hit his pinky, and the knob simultaneously. This causes the umpire to be momentarily confused as he hears *wood* and, at the same time, sees the batter crying in pain. Simultaneous contact does not mean the hitter is awarded first base! The ball must strike the batter or his clothing *prior* to the bat. However, in the case of the "double-hit," the official will usually award the hitter first base. Why? Why not? If the guy's pinky is bruised or broken, you're going to look mighty silly claiming it didn't hit him.

This leads us to the topic of the pitch actually hitting the batter or his clothing in the strike zone. It is difficult enough to distinguish a ball from a strike under perfect viewing conditions, let alone when the batter is taking away your normal perspective. I'm not kidding! It might look easy on the "Game of the Week," but it's quite a different story when a slider busts over at more than 90 mph. It is a very normal reaction for the umpire to award the hitter first when he *has* been hit with a pitch—anywhere. Sometimes, being too technical can incite a team to become irreversibly annoyed with you. They remember you as the umpire who is technical for life! To avoid this constant affiliation, good common sense should prevail.

Please do not get the impression that I am suggesting that if a hitter intentionally leans into the strike zone to be hit, that the umpire should go along with it. Absolutely not! I'd call it in a flash. The same goes if he stands his ground, not trying to avoid the pitch. However, I am saying that if the batter's act is borderline, it would be better for both teams and the umpires to rule as everyone *sees*—"Hits batsman, first base." At times, it is more intelligent to rule on how things appear, rather than try to over dissect the play and end up with a surprisingly controversial ruling.

In or Out of Batter's Box
Rule 6.03

The majority of spectators who attend ballgames have one thing in common. They view the game *minus* objectivity. It is quite understandable, and we don't slight them for this. Before I became a professional umpire I always wanted my team to win— period! Fans pay their money to see and root for their team. For the same money, they are permitted to berate umpires at will, at a surprisingly uninhibited level.

Diehard fans accuse umpires of cheating, sleeping, blindness, etc., etc. The list is endless. One of the most common observations they make is when a batter appears to be out of the confines of the batter's box. Until the lime chalk lines become obliterated by the game's length and constant activity around the home plate area, the fans can usually determine if a hitter is in the box or not. If, in the fan's mind the batsman is violating the rule, the umpire can expect to hear all about it.

Fans, we appreciate the assistance. However, there are a couple of baseball facts you may not be in touch with. The batter's foot or

In or Out of Batter's Box
Rule 6.03

6.03 The batter's legal position shall be with both feet within the batter's box.

APPROVED RULING: The lines defining the box are within the batter's box.

feet *on* the line does not mean "the hitter is out of the box." His shoes may be positioned on the line. Even though he may have only a minute portion of his shoe on the line, he will still be considered within the legal confines of the box.

Now, there are occasions when the hitter does have one foot or the other completely out of the box. It would only make sense to have the umpire, at this time, direct the hitter to legalize his position. This might sound unreasonable, but this is one time where the umpire does not necessarily want to exercise his authority. Not logical? Permit me to explain.

Most teams usually have one or two players who take their natural batting position with the back foot a few inches behind the back line of the box. Why? It is their most comfortable position. Then why does the umpire dismiss the opportunity to enforce the rule? Good question. If the plate umpire can see the infraction, you can bet the catcher is aware of it, too. The umpire will not direct the batter to move up *unless* the catcher asks him to get the hitter in the box. Usually, the catcher *will not* make such a request, because that will set a precedent for everyone to conform—including his own teammates! The extra few inches that allow comfort to the hitter are not that significant in the final outcome of his turn at bat. Therefore, by the catcher prompting an official commitment from the umpire, he is, in turn, creating similar consequences for his teammates, as well.

So now our umpire is listening to all the fans giving him the business about the hitter being out of the box...and they're right! What to do? Absolutely nothing! It is an unwritten rule that creates no problem for the participants on the field. If and when one team protests the technicality, the umpire can easily justify his insistence by passing the buck on the catcher and keep his own fair play reputation intact.

Ball Hits Batter out of the Batter's Box
Batter's Interference
Rule 6.05G

Batter's interference (see illustration) is one of the toughest calls to make for a number of reasons. In making this call the umpire must be thoroughly convinced the ball touched the batter *outside* of the box. There is only a split second to see the contact, and the ensuing movements of both the hitter and catcher can obstruct the umpire's vision.

As a young professional umpire, I was unaware of some of the game's "unwritten rules." I was fully aware of the game's written rules and would abide by them religiously. I felt it was my duty to rule on every technicality that came into play, rather than overlook some of them. I didn't even know how to overlook them. I had a lot to learn, and did so the hard way.

One of my most consistent rhubarbs was this batter's interference. For some reason, unknown to me at the time, I would see and call more batters out for interference than any umpire in the league. In retrospect, I now realize the cause of my flair for controversy. I was simply too technical my first two years in the

179

Ball Hits Batter Out of Batter's Box
Batter's Interference
Rule 6.05 (g)

6.05 A batter is out when—

(g) His fair ball touches him before touching a fielder.

180

game (1975–76). By no means am I admitting to missing the calls. On the contrary! However, I needed to learn to let the players play *their* game. My job was to *follow* the game as closely as possible without looking for trouble. Even after I did learn to be more lenient, trouble still *found me!*

Any part of the body that touches the ball in fair territory is grounds for interference. No two ways about it. The trouble is, however, in having the players and managers believe that. I have said it before and I'll say it again: "Sometimes umpires must rule on how it looks, rather than the way it is." This play is a perfect example.

By having one foot out of the box, the batter has now placed himself in jeopardy of being called out if the ball touches him. Therefore, it is a good idea to make him be *completely* out of the box to justify your call. It is much simpler for everyone to believe if the batter is *noticeably* out of the box. But, calling him out when he is on the borderline, will most definitely create havoc. I'm sure of it, because I called it enough times to know. When I started calling the borderline infractions a *foul ball* there was little or no argument. Everybody was happy and left me alone. This left me with very little to do other than gloat over my newly acquired judgment. Why look for trouble? No one else does! Sure, I might have heard a voice or a single criticism out of the dugout, but overall the less I called the batter out, the less the game was interrupted with a heated argument.

My advice here is, again, not to be too technical on this play. After awhile you know when to call it because the play can almost call itself. Making sure that the batter is noticeably out of the box, before calling him out, saves precious time and a tag of being too technical. If it's close, or you're just not sure, call it foul! I wish it was that easy for me when I broke in.

Thrown Batting Helmet
Rule 6.05 H 6th paragraph

Runners are advised to wear their helmets even while circling the bases. But have you ever had a batting helmet on? It's like being on the beach, with a sea shell up to your ear. The helmet is distracting and inhibiting to some runners, and a ballplayer is apt to feel freer and looser after somehow discarding it, thinking to himself, "Who cares if the throw splits my head open, the fans will give me a standing ovation." It could very easily fall off during a moment's surge of speed or an abrupt halt. But, a quick slap on the brim can put an end to the misery, as well.

Taking all this into consideration, the umpire must weigh the evidence. Should the runner be given the benefit of the doubt. After all, the umpire might feel the runner lacked intent to interfere with the rolling ball. It could be completely accidental and unintentional. I've put myself in the runner's shoes at times, and understand his dilemmas.

But the rules of baseball specifically mention that protective helmets must be *worn* by runners and hitters. This problem was created by our tricky batter-runner. He's got to be called out, for this intentional or unintentional interference. This act was unnatural to the base-running guidelines and, therefore, if a fielder must change direction because of a thrown helmet, the runner must pay.

Thrown Batting Helmet
Rule 6.05 (h)

6.05 (h) A batter is out when—

If, in the umpire's judgment, there is intent on the part of a baserunner to interfere with a batted or thrown ball by dropping the helmet or throwing it at the ball, then the runner would be out, the ball dead and runners would return to last base legally touched.

Accidental Helmet Interference
6.05 H 4th paragraph

In contrast to a runner who actively and knowingly removes his protective helmet from his head, our umpiring crew must be equally alert for pure "acts of God," as we call them in the trade.

Of course, anytime the ball reacts unnaturally or turns up in an unorthodox location, one manager or the other is going to try to turn it to his advantage.

I have to be honest with you by first telling you I have never once seen the helmet cover a live ball (or a dead one for that matter), but I certainly consider the possibility of this happening quite feasible. Why not? Crazier things have happened. Remember in baseball the most widely used expression is "you never know."

But the lords of baseball's Rules Committees have carefully ruled on eminently surprising moments, and this is clearly one of them. On this play, the catcher must adjust to adversity as he's done on countless occasions. This apparently easy play has turned into a nightmarish farce.

Accidental Helmet Interference
Rule 6.05 (h)

6.05 (h) In cases where the batting helmet is accidentally hit with a batted or thrown ball, the ball remains in play the same as if it has not hit the helmet.

If a batted ball strikes a batting helmet or any other object foreign to the natural ground while on foul territory, it is a foul ball and the ball is dead.

The umpire must be correct in determining whether the ball was obstructed in fair or foul territory, and indicate his decision aggressively and immediately. On a ball very close to the foul line, the catcher will most likely argue the point that the ball was indeed foul when touched by the helmet (that is if he failed to field it). After learning that the ball is alive and in play, he will be further infuriated to realize there was no interference.

The umpire will reign again as master tactician. Our umpire will confirm his rebuttal by clearly stating that he had straddled the baseline and was in perfect position to judge the ball's roll. If need be, he also will add that he was positioned to judge the helmet-ball contact even if the contact was made in mid-air, as again straddling the baseline would give him the exact view he would need to create an imaginary baseline plane, vertically. In any case, it's a unique call as both umpire's judgment and rule interpretation must be processed through his brain within seconds.

Running out of the Baseline
Rule 7.08A

To call a runner out for leaving the baseline should be one of the easiest calls an umpire has to make. While it is, only after considerable experience can an official master the art of recognizing this play.

Picture this situation: Runner on first, less than two out and a slow grounder is hit to the second baseman. Let's start with the thought process of the second baseman: It's going to be tough to get two here. No time to flip to second (for the shortstop covering), then relay to first. My move is to charge the ball, tag the runner myself, then quickly whip it to first to complete the D.P. Perfectly sane reasoning. Now let's examine the runner's thoughts: No chance to make second safely—he'll easily force me. My only chance is to lure him into trying to tag me, then swerve to avoid the tag—can't go out of the base-line or I'll be called out— must dart out of his line at the last possible moment and hope to make him miscalculate and miss the apparently easy tag and therefore use up enough time to make him rush his throw to first. All sound reasoning on both players' parts.

Now, let me tell you what our second base or infield umpire is doing and thinking. If a two-man umpire system is in effect, the base umpire will have to call both ends of the play, which detracts from his concentration in order of sequence. But for argument's sake let's put four umpires out there, and with this situation in mind, the second base ump has only the responsibility of the lead runner approaching second base.

The first thing he will do to react to this play is turn and face the ball and the upcoming force. He sees the second baseman charging, the runner approaching, and the ball nearing its entrapment. All three are arriving at approximately the same place at the same time. Our wide-eyed ump now realizes the infielder is going to go for the runner. He must get in position to witness the tag. It's going to be quick and neat, and most likely the runner will veer. The ump moves laterally for position to determine if any daylight will come between the outstretched glove and the runner's body. The ump's eyes are focused directly on this aspect. He must clearly see this tag! In addition, the umpire must be aware of the possibility that this tricky little second sacker might try to *tag with his glove,* and leave the ball in his throwing hand to save the time in transferring the ball, therefore saving a precious half-second needed on the back end of the D.P. Our umpire has concluded he will absolutely not miss the moment of truth that needs the utmost certainty. There it is—he missed him!! "Safe, you missed him," he shouts. Now the infielder, with no hope but to fire to first to salvage one out, does exactly that. Let's say he's out at first. Play's over—except for the ensuing argument. The umpire's thinking, "Why are they charging at me; he knows he missed the tag, I'm positive of that! Here comes that feisty little manager. What the hell could he have to say, he was 150 feet from the play."

After the umpire has reviewed his decision in his own mind, his head is clearing to make room for the screaming voices around him.

"Hey, what the hell game are you watching, the guy was out of the baselines!! Of course I missed the tag, he ran out of the baselines! I had no chance. You let him run out out there!" Our

Running Out of the Baseline
Rule 7.08 (a)

7.08 Any runner is out when—

(a) (1) He runs more than three feet away from a direct line between bases to avoid being tagged, unless his action is to avoid interference with a fielder fielding a batted ball; or (2) after touching first base, he leaves the baseline, obviously abandoning his effort to touch the next base.

official thinks back 20 seconds ago and does faintly remember the runner veering slightly inside, squirming to pass untouched to the salvation of second. Could he have run out of the baseline? I'm not sure. I ruled him safe, now am I to reverse it because they brought it to my attention? What was I thinking about? Now could I forget to look for that? Do I now ask for help from my colleagues? No! How could they possibly have had a better look than I, when I'm right here on top of the play? Besides, it's my call not theirs.

"Look, you guys," our ump summarizes," the runner avoided the tag with a body fake and your man missed the tag. In my judgment he didn't leave the baseline. Let's go!" Sure, what else is he going to say? "I didn't consider the possibility because I was looking for the tag?" This exact situation happened to me a number of times, until I became accustomed to the events that could transpire ... and the importance of looking for both, as well. I did finally come up with an aid to guide me. There is almost no way that a runner can evade a tag unless he alters his route at the time the fielder extends his arm to apply the tag. In doing so, he is trying to avoid the contact. If he runs three feet out of a direct line between bases, he's out! Simple. Three feet is a very small area of leniency to control. Besides, no one is going to bring out a ruler to measure his spike marks. Therefore, the umpire's judgment is simplified somewhat. In looking for the tag, if he sees the runner avoid it by re-routing his path, he can easily justify his "out of baseline" ruling by claiming it was obvious he ran more than three feet out of line, period. Why complicate matters by trying to be exact? It's almost impossible. Next case.

Intentional Interference
Rule 7.08B - 7.09F

This unusual baseball play took place in the 1978 World Series. The series participants were the Los Angeles Dodgers and New York Yankees. The play in question caused several eyebrows to be raised by fans, the media, and most of all the screaming L.A. club. (We will skip the game promo and buildup by eliminating game number, city, starting pitcher, inning, etc., etc...)

Reggie Jackson, the Yankee's perennial star, was on first base, Thurman Munson on second with less than two out. A hard smash was dealt to Dodger's shortstop Russell for an apparently easy D.P. The ball was hit so sharply that Jackson was left with no chance either to reach second safely ahead of the force or to break up the D.P. He was simply a Yankee uniform in between bases. The easy relay to Steve Garvey, the Dodger first baseman was just a formality at this point. Reggie had other ideas, however. The relay that hit Jackson in the hip was ruled unintentional, and the runner safe at first. This brought Garvey and Dodger manager Tommy Lasorda to a rage, and they both insisted the contact on Jackson's part was intentional. Frank Pulli, the first base umpire, in debate with Garvey and Lasorda (and a few other interested parties) argued with a vehemence that belied his doubt, the same doubt that I have felt in crucial situations. However, the pressure in a World Series must be unimaginable.

I can clearly remember watching the game on TV and seeing the relay about three times—something Pulli could not do! To be perfectly honest, I must admit a feeling of compassion when in my judgment, Jackson HAD intentionally interfered with the relay. I just thought Frank didn't see it! I was trying to imagine how Frank was stating his case and validating his call.

I believe Frank never saw the actual "bump and deflect" routine. If Pulli was indeed preparing to see the back end of the D.P. properly, he would be facing the bag, and not watching the ball as it is approaching the base, or Jackson. No one follows a double play relay in mid-air, for 90 feet. After it leaves the thrower's hand you estimate the height, turn and watch the bag, the runner and the first baseman and wait for the ball.

Pulli took part in a television interview the day after the game. The network ran the replay in slow motion for the viewing audience and Pulli. Frank again repeated his call by saying he didn't see Reggie intentionally move into it. I certainly did!

My opinion of the play was, and still is, this: Jackson realized he had no chance to break up the D.P. He was actually closer to first base than he was to second. On following the flight of the relay, Reggie was inclined to slightly deflect the ball by popping his hip out to his right, as he was only inches from it anyway, just lingering between bases. A slight obstruction would kill the chance of a D.P. Jackson completed his play expertly enough to not bring attention to himself. Most people viewing the game in person probably were surprised the ball never reach Garvey and reasoned that the ball hit Jackson inadvertently along the way— exactly what Jackson wanted everyone to believe, most of all, Mr. Pulli.

Frank realized a D.P. was in order and, as the play developed, he moved into the conventional position for attacking this play (some 5 to 10 feet off the line in fair territory trying to attain a 90°

Intentional Interference
Rule 7.08 (b) - 7.09 (f)

7.08 Any runner is out when—

(b) He intentionally interferes with a thrown ball; or hinders a fielder attempting to make a play on a batted ball;

7.09 It is interference by a batter or a runner when—

(f) Any batter or runner who has just been put out hinders or impedes any following play being made on a runner. Such runner shall be declared out for the interference of his teammate.

angle on the action—not the best spot to be battling these circumstances considering what actually happened. If he were in foul territory looking at Jackson's rear end, he might have had a better opportunity to catch the hip action. Pulli cannot be accused of having bad position, as his choice of weapons was excellent . . . under normal circumstances. So Pulli gets his angle, watches shortstop Bill Russell fire to first, and naturally turns to wait for the routine out at first. Pow!! No ball, and they're mad as hell! You know something's up. In my opinion, there was no way Pulli had Jackson in the picture, nor was he expecting anything but a play at first.

When the Dodgers argued, it was clear they were pleading with Pulli to ask second base umpire Joe Brinkman for his help. Whether Pulli asked or not, would not have been conclusive. Brinkman has one job and one job only on this play—everything that happens at second. That includes the aftermath of the force. In most cases during double plays there is contact at the bag where the ump must be on the lookout for foul play by the hard-sliding runner. To add to these responsibilities, he must also rule on the pivot man touching the base and controlling the ball. (On this particular play, Brinkman had to make an additional call on Russell's intent to catch the original line drive. Russell did drop the hard smash, and it was up to Brinkman's judgment to decide if the dropped ball was intentional or not. If he had ruled it intentional the play would have been called dead, the batter out, and Jackson would remain at 1st.) Brinkman is focusing on second base and the play's follow-through. He was most probably unaware of Jackson's unorthodox baserunning. Second base umpires usually turn to the back end of the play right about the time the ball is getting to first and are not set to call "that play." Therefore, they are not able to make a true determination of the play.

This brings us to the other two umpires, home plate and third base. Forget the third base umpire, he's about 150 feet away. He couldn't possibly tell if Jackson did anything or not. The plate umpire is about 100 feet away, but has no angle to bring him to any clear judgment on Jackson's body movements. Any mini-movement from left to right would not appear substantial from home plate.

So Pulli has to die with this call one way or the other. It is a very unusual predicament and one I can relate to instinctively. I believe I would have ruled precisely the same if I had taken the same position as did Pulli (usually on a D.P., I would utilize the infield cutout around first base. It gives you a great view of the play at first, but would be an even worse spot to be in to rule on the "Jackson play."

Sometimes, even a well-positioned umpire may not see clearly when an unusual play arises. I do not recommend admitting "not seeing the play." I suggest reasoning not to have been entirely positive, because of unforeseen circumstances. A meeting of the umpires at this point would have been in order, not necessarily to change the call, but at least to have a better understanding of all the official opinions on the play before finalizing the decision.

Making the Turn Toward Second

Rule 7.08J

The rule book suggests that the best way to umpire a ballgame is to keep your eye everlastingly on the ball. No doubt about it! However, rules are made to be broken . . . or in this case, improvised on.

Baserunners who have reached first base safely are not in the habit of trying to advance to second, unless the ball has gone astray. When the throw does get by the first sacker, natural instinct comes into play. The first person to react will be the first base coach. He will almost surely vocalize his delight by yelling to the runner, "Go, go, take second!" In most cases the coach will be correct in his judgment, but occasionally it will backfire because the ball will either be snared by the second baseman or catcher backing up the play, or by a direct rebound to one of them off the fence or wall behind first. Now the coach has to bark out restaining orders that will probably be too late.

The batter-runner was instinctively running with everything he had to reach first safely. He was probably aware that the ball had

Making the Turn Toward Second
Rule 7.08 (j)

7.08 Any runner is out when—

(j) He fails to return at once to first base after overrunnng or oversliding that base. If he attempts to run to second he is out when tagged. If, after overrunning or oversliding first base he starts toward the dugout, or toward his position, and fails to return to first base at once, he is out, on appeal, when he or the base is tagged.

eluded the grasp of the first baseman, but not until after he had run some 10 to 15 feet past the bag. Upon hearing the coach, and wanting to take advantage of the opportunity to claim an extra base, he will undoubtedly move or turn his body toward second base. Why not? He's got no time to lose. Every step and second is important.

The umpire has additional responsibility at this time. He must, of course, keep his eyes on the ball, and also be aware of the runner's intentions. By turning toward the infield, the runner has not *by this alone* made an attempt to go to second. He must make definite physical move in that direction. In most cases when the runner has been confused at the last moment, he will probably try to hold back his already established move toward second. Now he has three options! He can continue to try for second, run as fast as he can to the safety of first without being tagged, or try his hand at acting. By this, I mean he can casually walk back to the bag as if he is in no jeopardy of being put out, indicating he made no attempt to go in the first place.

I have ruled on this play countless times and one thought never eludes me. Will the defense argue my decision? Nine times out of 10 the defense will make the appeal for the purpose of influencing ruling in their favor. This is especially true when the whole dugout is crying "Tag him, tag him, he made a turn!" As an umpire, you must be strong in your own conception of what did actually take place. If the umpire did not see the runner's movements beyond the bag, he will undoubtedly become confused. Why is everyone yelling to tag him? Did he make the turn? Within two seconds the appeal will be made and he has to declare his decision. It is imperative that once the ball has gone wild, the umpire continue to look in both directions to see any spectator interference, dead ball territory and if the runner did indeed commit himself.

This is a tough decision to make as both teams will be looking for the decision to go their way. Players and managers are not experts on the rules and their strong desire to win influences their level of objectivity. With experience, an umpire can realize the situation immediately and therefore observe all possibilities, to rule on this play consistently and correctly.

Runner Overslides First Base and Ends up in Fair Territory
Rule 7.08C

I am not aware of the time period when sliding creatively became instrumental to baseball. I have to assume it didn't come about right off the *bat* (not originally intended, but a cute pun nevertheless). I say this because upon researching this book I was fortunate to be able to dissect the old scriptures written for the game. I determined that the degree of sophistication at that time (1800s) was not high. In any case, I am sure that sliding into first is rarer than a suicide squeeze. If I had not personally seen the play I have illustrated for you here, I would always have thought that this exact call would be an astronomically unlikely occurrence.

One of today's fortunate young umpires to make it to *The Show* recently is one Rick Reed. Rick now umpires in the A.L. I only know Rick from the few times we've crossed paths through the years, yet I like Rick and consider him more than an acquaintance. Rick and I started out in the minors at about the same time, when days off were far and few between. Days off are even more rare than a squeeze play and head-first dive into first combined, but somehow I managed to be seated in a Midwest League ballpark taking in a playoff game in 1975. The Midwest League is Class A baseball. That is relevant, because if not for lack of experience among all concerned, this call would have been reversed or, for that matter, never made in the first place.

Rick was working first base as the batter hit a ground ball to the left side of the infield. The infielder realized he needed to get off a quick, accurate throw to beat the batter-runner. As the play continued to develop, the runner, realizing he had the opportunity to beat the throw, dove head first at the bag and beat the ball. By the time he finished his slide (he did touch the bag on his way through) he was 8 to 10 feet beyond the bag, lying in fair territory! Rick ruled him safe, correctly. However, the first baseman, with nothing to lose, walked over and put a formal tag on the fearless baserunner. Rick then proceeded to call him out!

From my seat, I swear, I initially agreed with Rick. What excellent timing and style I thought. The runner begged to differ and so did the Quad Cities manager, Bobby Knoop. It then hit me that Rick (and I) had been taken in by the unusual position of the baserunner. Rick must have thought as did I, ''Hey, this guy's in fair territory, he's off the base and just been tagged. He's got to be called out.'' I can offer my feelings of sympathy as I had thought exactly as Rick did, at the time. However, with a few moments to ponder my thoughts, I reversed my decision as I was sure Rick would do shortly. The relevance did not lie on which side of the foul line the baserunner was occupying. This has no bearing on the decision—or at least shouldn't have.

As the argument continued, I became aware that Knoop was arguing in vain.

Rick was not about to change his initial decision. Bobby Knoop was the fairest manager in the league. He would almost never argue with umpires and even when he did, it was done calmly and with gentlemanly diplomacy. In this trade we call it *respect*. This time was no exception, as Bobby held his composure and tried reasoning with Rick. No dice! The call stood! I was mesmerized. I just know Rick had to be confused at some point during the argument if indeed he was correct. Evidently, he concluded that the rule was either one or the other (the runner was still safe or was

**Runner Overslides First Base and Ends
Up in Fair Territory
Rule 7.08 (c)**

7.08 Any runner is out when—

(c) He is tagged, when the ball is alive, while off his base. EXCEPTION: A batter-runner cannot be tagged out after overrunning or oversliding first base if he returns immediately to the base.

now out). He picked out. I did not see a consultation between the game's officials. Perhaps this would have cleared things up, *or* confused another umpire. Umpires are less pliable when they're in the low minors. At this stage of a career it is difficult to admit the truth to yourself when you are wrong or in doubt. That results in less umpire communication through mid-game conferences.

Rick Reed is now a bona fide professional umpire, and surely a lot wiser, as well. He works daily with major leaguers who have been occasionally embarrassed in front of a greater amount of people than one could possibly tabulate. When one becomes an umpire, from that moment on he forfeits the right to be innocent until proven guilty. A majority of controversial decisions are viewed by the players and fans without objectivity. Therefore, the umpire is singled out as the villian. Umpires and umpires alone can rationalize a seemingly one-sided decision, because of their training, rule interpretations and insight. They are paid to take the short end of the stick—even when they are right. And when they are wrong, they have to live with it like no other (except other umpires) can imagine.

Bunted Ball Hits Dropped Bat
Rule 6.05H

Remember when you were a kid (or if you're a kid now) and you were always destined to be the game's catcher? Weren't you thrilled to be given the opportunity to have your friends throw their bats wildly after their trimphant hits? Ah, the pain! Wasn't it great? How about when you specifically told them right before they stepped in to hit, "Hey, man, don't throw the bat!" It was like pushing the automatic button that read *Throw Bat Directly at Catcher!* The warning never helped, as the chronic bat flingers never learned . . . until the catcher broke their discarded bats.

Finally, our friends became young adults and gained control of their annoying and dangerous habits. They began dropping their bats nicely around the home plate area, never once imagining they were in jeopardy of interfering with their destiny.

From my experience, I can tell you that it is highly unlikely that a hitter would actually consider having his bat perform "double duty" by using his dropped bat to make an apparently easy play turn into a work of art. As mentioned in Rule 6.05H, a ball rolling

**Bunted Ball Hits Dropped Bat
Rule 6.05 (h)**

6.05 A batter is out when—

(h) After hitting or bunting a fair ball, his bat hits the ball a second time in fair territory. The ball is dead and no runners may advance. If the batter-runner drops his bat and the ball rolls against the bat in fair territory and, in the umpire's judgment, there was no intention to interfere with the course of the ball, the ball is alive and in play.

in fair territory that is deflected off its course by a motionless bat on the ground would be alive and in play. This means that a ball could be deflected from fair territory into foul and therefore be ruled foul. If the ball was initially rolling in foul territory and eventually rolled up to touch the stationary bat, the ball would be ruled *foul* immediately. In other words, the relative position of the ball when contacting the bat is significant. It's live in fair territory and foul if touched in foul territory.

How about if the bat is still rolling at the time of contact? This is when the plate umpire must call upon his precise judgment. If indeed the bat is moving, the batter is out, whether it's intentional or not. Some players, after bunting, carry their lumber a considerable distance before dropping it. There is no penalty for doing so. As a matter of fact, there is no rule that prevents a batter-runner from carrying his cherished club all the way around the bases if he wants . . . as long as he does not cause interference by doing so. (Players are in love with their bats, yet I haven't seen anyone go to *that* extreme to protect their sentimental attachments.)

What is truly amazing to me is that the oddest predicaments occur in and around the home plate area. You think you've seen everything until something new crosses in front of your eyes. I've sat up long into many nights contemplating hypothetical baseball situations. I would prepare rulings to coincide with each knotty problem and be proud of my insight and ambition, only to go out on the field and see something I hadn't imagined. Baseball is a funny game and always changing, as its players and managers are deliberately or inadvertently creating new and unheard of calamities.

Runner on Base Unintentionally Interferes With Fielder

Rule 7.08B

Determining whether an *act* on a baseball field is interference or not is most difficult for an umpire. In making the decision one way or the other, he must react in less than two seconds. That is a relatively short period of time for one to consider all the facts, rule expertly, then award bases correctly.

When players or the ball are interfered with, it is quite normal for one to immediately admit a touch of doubt. An umpire must be absolutely sure that he first saw the play clearly, then replay the act in his head as quickly as he possibly can in order to take proper action. An extra second of time is a great help in puting things in proper perspective. This is an especially good idea for the illustrated situation shown pertaining to rule 7.08B.

The first thing that base coaches relay to new arrivals at their bases is a reminder of the baserunning tactics that will be employed on upcoming line drives, grounders and fly balls. The score, outs and overall defense contribute to the strategy. With a runner on third, less than two outs and a ground ball to the left side, the odds are that the runner will *not* try to score. He will hold third and hope the next guy can drive him in. The runner is entitled to retreat as long as he does not interfere with the ball or fielder in doing so. The 15-inch-square base is his only hope of safety and rightfully his until a force play arises. If the ball was to hit him while he was on base or returning to the base (in fair territory), he would be out, with no questions asked. If he was to interfere with the third baseman before he got back to his base, then he would again be out for not giving the fielder the space needed to make the play. A smart third baseman would angle in toward the runner and try to have the runner crash into him while he was returning.

However, the rules do permit the runner to have some peace of mind while on the basepaths. If he is definitely on his base, and not trying to create adversity, the fielder will have to work around him. In this case, the umpire will have to take particular note of the runner's intent: He could appear to be unaware of the problem at hand, but at the same time create the problem. Ballplayers, in general, do not think along those lines in split-second situations. In any case, the umpire must position himself to see everything. By that, I mean the man in blue has more to consider than just interference . . . what about fair or foul? With the ball very close to the line, our official must make this decision by remaining on the line and, in addition, make sure he does not interfere himself by getting in too close to the play or by letting the ball deflect off him.

No matter what, you can bet this play will bring out the tempers of the third baseman and his manager. They will insist that they were interfered with. When the umpire explains that it is not interference because the runner was on his base, they will undoubtedly claim he was *not* . . . and add that he did it intentionally, to boot! I'm sure of it! I've had players tell me they didn't swing when I called an attempted half-swing on them for a strike; however, had they made contact, they would have driven the ball 300 feet.

Keep in mind the position of the runner when he is returning. Bases are located in fair territory and only on the run to first is a

**Runner on Base Unintentionally Interferes With Fielder
Rule 7.08 (b)**

7.08 Any runner is out when—

(b) He intentionally interferes with a thrown ball; or hinders a fielder attempting to make a play on a batted ball;

A runner who is adjudged to have hindered a fielder who is attempting to make a play on a batted ball is out whether it was intentional or not.

If, however, the runner has contact with a legally occupied base when he hinders the fielder, he shall not be called out unless, in the umpire's judgment, such hindrance, whether it occurs on fair or foul territory, is intentional. If the umpire declares the hindrance intentional, the following penalty shall apply: With less than two out, the umpire shall declare both the runner and batter out. With two out, the umpire shall declare the batter out.

208

three-foot lane constructed for the traffic there. At third, there is no three-foot lane. It would look strange if he ran back to third in fair territory, but oddly enough this is not grounds for interference. The point here is to consider if he was *actually on base*. According to the illustration, he has clearly made it back (I should know, I created it!). The runner is quite naturally protecting his head as any of us would in his predicament. The call stands . . . he's safe!

Batter Intentionally Deflects the Course of a Foul Ball
Rule 6.05 I

The immediate question raised in reviewing this rule is why would a runner intentionally kick, touch or deflect a foul ball? It's a good question, but not a great one.

It has been noted by authorized sports observers that baseball players or any athletes participating in sports competition do not always act within the scope of pure logic. Therefore, I understand their insistence on creating adversity in hopes of succeeding as a result of it.

Clearly interfering, with intent is, by and large, a no-no in any sport. Baseball is no exception, so of course an immediate time-out is indicated by the official. Players realize their intent, but absolutely hate to admit it at the time. It is within the rules to have a ball ultimately ruled *fair* after it has bounded around in foul territory. Bearing this in mind, the batter-runner may choose to exercise his option to alter fate as he may believe the ball will continue to roll, curving back into fair territory, giving the catcher an easy play for a putout.

**Batter Intentionally Deflects the Course
of a Foul Ball
Rule 6.05 (i)**

6.05 A batter is out when—

(i) After hitting or bunting a foul ball, he intentionally deflects the course of the ball in any manner while running to first base. The ball is dead and no runners may advance.

The umpire must maintain a firm position here because as positive as he claims to be, the runner will stipulate that he was merely trying to save everyone time or make up some other story. He will go as far as claiming that "Yes, it was intentional, but not to kill the catcher's chances, as the ball was obviously foul." Good story; however, there is one flaw in it: A batted ball does not become foul until it either comes to a complete stop or is touched by a fielder.

Interference calls always carry a certain amount of pressure. They are inning-killers and create serious and long *arguments*. I hope we can close the book on this *one*.